The Red Menace

How Lipstick Changed the Face of American History

Ilise S. Carter

Prometheus Books

Guilford, Connecticut

PB Prometheus Books

An imprint of The Rowman & Littlefield Publishing Group, Inc.
4501 Forbes Blvd., Ste. 200
Lanham, MD 20706
www.rowman.com

Distributed by NATIONAL BOOK NETWORK

British Library Cataloguing in Publication Information Available

Library of Congress Cataloging-in-Publication Data

Names: Carter, Ilise S., 1973– author.
Title: The red menace : how lipstick changed the face of American history / by Ilise S. Carter.
Description: Lanham, MD : Prometheus Books, [2021] | Includes bibliographical references and index. | Summary: "In America, lipstick is the foundation of empires; it's a signature of identity; it's propaganda, self-expression, oppression, freedom, and rebellion. It's a multi-billion-dollar industry and one of our most iconic accessories of gender. This engaging and entertaining history of lipstick in America throughout the twentieth century and into the present will give readers a new view of the little tube's big place in modern America; marching with the Suffragettes, building Fortune 500 businesses, being present at Stonewall, and engineered for space travel"— Provided by publisher.
Identifiers: LCCN 2021017416 (print) | LCCN 2021017417 (ebook) | ISBN 9781633887107 (cloth) | ISBN 9781633887114 (epub)
Subjects: LCSH: Lipstick—United States—History. | Lipstick—United States—Social aspects. | Women—Social life and customs—United States.
Classification: LCC GT2340 .C37 2021 (print) | LCC GT2340 (ebook) | DDC 391.6/3—dc23
LC record available at https://lccn.loc.gov/2021017416
LC ebook record available at https://lccn.loc.gov/2021017417

♾️™ The paper used in this publication meets the minimum requirements of American National Standard for Information Sciences—Permanence of Paper for Printed Library Materials, ANSI/NISO Z39.48-1992.

For my dad,
Maurice "Marty" Carter, MD,
engineer, orthopedist, husband, father, friend,
bon vivant, dandy, and mensch

CONTENTS

CHAPTER ONE

RED COATS OF ANOTHER SORT
The Colonies to the Civil War

Shades of the Decade
Martha Washington's Finest Lip Salve in the World
Rouge

L et's start with the legend: according to the corporate mythology, in 1912[1] the iconic cosmetics impresario Elizabeth Arden handed out red lipstick to suffragettes as they marched down Manhattan's Fifth Avenue demanding the vote. They instantly took to the bold pop of color and added a bright lip to their look. Thus, freed from the constraints of its association with sex workers, fancy feminist ladies rebranded lipstick as a glamorous form of rebellion, making lip color essential for every woman, and the rest is beauty history.

Except when it isn't. It's a great story and it does have some threads of truth to it (Arden did march in at least one parade), but it's not the whole story of how we came to be one nation under gloss. However, the subject being American history, you have to start somewhere, and generally speaking we like to start with one big event: "the shot heard round the world"; "now he belongs to the ages"; "a day that will live in infamy." Unfortunately, in addressing the question of lipstick and its place in American history, there's no one bright flash of inspiration. Instead it's a long winding chain of events, personalities, and inventions intertwined with race, class, commerce, media, and gender that starts before America was even these United States; indeed, before lipstick was even in stick form.

Lipstick, or lip color, in the 1700s and 1800s would have been known as lip rouge or just rouge in its earliest, all-purpose form and wouldn't come in a stick shape until the late nineteenth century and the metal tube that we're familiar with until 1917. It was available in two formulas: rouge in powder—just what it sounds like—or pomatum or salve, which mixed a red dye with some sort of emollient. Thus, the name *rouge* from the French word for red. The color was limited to the red family and derived from either vegetable dyes or, more commonly, carmine (also known as cochineal), which is ground beetle shells. Using it was less about personal expression or following trends and more about trying to re-create or enhance the natural blush of youth. Use of color occurred but probably sparingly for most American women due to the fact that the country was still something of a frontier, and there was little call for it in rural areas and work-a-day life.

Little but not none. For example, in 1766—the same year that the English parliament passed the American Colonies Act, which formalized its full governmental sovereignty over the upstart backwater on the other side of the Atlantic—one "Ann Pearson, Milliner," took out an advertisement in Benjamin Franklin's *Pennsylvania Gazette* to offer the consumers of Philadelphia imported "rouge" and "lip salve,"[2] in addition to other dainties. The fact that those toiletry items share a page with advertising for "fine Liverpool beer," "almanacks" with a "ladies' form of prayer for a husband," a horse race, and a $3 reward for the return of a runaway "negro wench"[3] places cosmetics firmly in the swirl of timeless American interests.

Ms. Pearson's offerings, though perhaps the height of chic for eighteenth-century Philadelphia, were not even particularly novel in the scheme of things. Adornment being a natural instinct, painting the body as an act of vanity or worship is probably one of the oldest forms of grooming. From the Egyptians, who buried their dead of both sexes with makeup palettes, to Queen Elizabeth I, who spackled over her smallpox scars with a white lead paste, coloring our skin has long been part of our lives. Held up as holy, denounced as profane, like every human habit, color cosmetics would arrive along with Europeans sooner or later. (That is, for the purpose of this discussion, putting aside the long-established painting rituals and practices of the indigenous societies who were already here. That's a separate story worthy of its own scholarship.)

It's hard to say exactly when cosmetics hit the shores of the Colonies, but it's safe to say they didn't arrive on the *Mayflower* with the Pilgrims. Nor did they hold much interest for the Puritans, who were so famously persnickety and fashion averse that simplicity of style was a matter of law. The Massachusetts Bay Colony enacted in its laws a literal fashion police clause forbidding "the great, superfluous, and unnecessary expenses occasioned by reason of new and immodest fashions."[4] Although legislators specified that fancy hatbands, long wigs, and "great sleeves" could land you in front of a judge, oddly there's no mention of cosmetics. It's hard to specifically say why this is; it's unlikely that the elders were okay with a bright pop of color paired with your understated black ensemble. It is possible it just hadn't come up yet. Makeup (which was expressly forbidden to their counterparts in Europe) was a highly impractical and luxurious contraband item for members of a religious sect trying to carve out its subsistence from an inhospitable wilderness wherein every last consumer item had to be grown, made, hunted, or imported at great expense.

As a lifestyle, however, basic black and stringent self-denial only goes so far for so many people. The Colonies, as a living, growing experiment in capitalism, religious freedom, and politics, would have to expand and adapt if they were to survive. To cut a long story short for the purpose of expediency, it's necessary only to know that during the intervening couple decades in American history, cities grew, farmland was tilled, a truly impressive victory was eked out against the British Empire, and a whole new set of rules was established that were concerned less with the size of its citizens' hatband and more with the lofty natural law ideals of the Enlightenment. (In theory, anyway.)

Though still a minor player in most women's dressing rituals, lip color boasts some early celebrity endorsements.

The original first lady Martha Washington had a recipe for what she immodestly described as "the finest lip salve in the world" that you could conceivably whip up on your own stove.

Take 2 ozs of Virgin Wax, 2 ozs best Hog's Lard, 1/2 an oz of Spermacetti [*sic*], 10 oz Oil of Sweet Almonds, 2 drachmas Balsam of Peru, 2 drachmas Alkanet Root, cut small, 6 new raisins of the sun dried small,

The *first* First Lady. Mrs. Washington was one of the countless American women who had her own homespun recipe for tinted lip balm. *NYPL Collection*

a little fine sugar—simmer them all a little while, then strain it off in little cups or ointment boxes of china.[5]

The result is a tinted lip balm containing humectants like spermaceti, a waxy substance harvested from whales' heads, and lard, sweetener, plus a sheer reddish coloring from the alkanet root. Primitive perhaps but entirely workable (not unlike the fledgling nation itself).

So lip color was available commercially and domestically, but how widespread was its use? In the absence of marketing data, it's hard to say exactly but enough that the popular press of the time (i.e., books, newspapers, and magazines) seemed split as to whether painting oneself was a good thing or a bad thing. In his *Letters to a Young Lady*, Reverend John Bennett advised against it as a form of deception, warning that "Blush, my dear girl, is such an unseemly practice. Be content to be what God and nature intended you: appear in your true colors, abhor any thing like deceit in your appearance as well as your character."[6] On the other hand, books of household hints like *The Compleat Toilet** also gave their own recipes for "Rouge in Powder"[7] for the trendy housewife in much the same way that modern fashion magazines offer beauty tips. There are several factors that fueled the mixed messaging here: social standing, religious conviction, financial aspiration, and gender roles—put another way, some of what would come to be America's greatest pop culture hits.

At the dawn of the American experiment, Abigail Adams admonished her husband, the future president John Adams, to "remember the ladies" and followed up with a powerful warning that "If particular care and attention is not paid to the ladies we are determined to foment a rebellion, and will not hold ourselves bound by any laws in which we have no voice, or representation."[8] Mr. Adams largely ignored her threats and the new republic lurched forward without women in government but not without their voices in popular culture. Attitudes about gender roles and what it was to be a woman in public—and in private—were forming in a way that would echo loudly through the following centuries.

An ingenue player on the world stage during the years between the British surrender in 1781 and the Civil War in 1860, America dedicated a lot of energy finding its feet as an independent cultural force. It had its first best-selling books, an ascendant free press, and even a teensy-weensy spot for women in the realm of public discourse. Tiny but present with writings aimed at women that tended to take the form of bodice-ripper "seduction novels" that offered romance but warned of the consequences of sex outside marriage (shame, death, ripping your best bodice) and housekeeping guides. There were, of course, women like poet Judith Sargent Murray asking if there was more to occupy the female mind than domestic tasks. Her 1790 essay "On the Equality of the Sexes" mused about the inherent cleverness of women and asked readers, "Is the needle and kitchen sufficient to employ the operations a soul such organized?"[9] It was a fair question but unfortunately not one that would get much traction the next century and a half or so. The main options offered to women would remain harlot or housewife.

---

* Go ahead and giggle, but we're talking about grooming rituals and not indoor plumbing, so pronounced *a la Française*: *toilette*.

On the housewife front, a white, working- and middle-class army of domesticity was being assembled. Hearth and home would be posited as the number one priority, and an endless number of cookbooks, household hints, magazines, and parenting guides would be put forth to help generations of women achieve the ideal. Even here women received mixed messages. There were both recipes for do-it-yourself lip salve, rouge, skin care, and the like, and missives against using cosmetics at all.

The arguments against makeup fell into two basic categories: (1) moral arguments (e.g., it's deceptive, un-American, unnatural, blasphemous, what have you) and (2) practical objections (e.g., it's bad for your skin; you aren't fooling anyone; it's poisonous). The latter had some merit in the century before the Food and Drug Administration was created. In the early part of the nineteenth century, the country hadn't exactly hit upon Manifest Destiny yet, and the beauty industry was already a proverbial Wild West of ingredients and promises. Lead, arsenic, and ethanol (then known as "spirit of wine") were chief among them, but without oversight and industry standards, there's no telling what other caustic ingredients made their way into the pots and boxes of color cosmetics and skin care; hog's lard and raisins might have been the best-case scenario.

Even as the federal government expanded its powers and commercial science rose to meet the cresting tide of the industrial revolution, there seemed to be no rush to protect female consumers from the perils and poisons of beauty. In 1839, the year of the *Amistad* uprising and the Trail of Tears, an editorial in the *Graham Journal of Health and Longevity* took the position that the regulation called for by a medical textbook was unnecessary on moral grounds and sexist notions about the foolishness of vanity.

> We differ from [*Dr. Smith's Anatomical Class Book*] when it calls for police regulation for the suppression of paint and cosmetics. Such regulations would cost more than enlighten the dupes of cosmetic follies. . . . No, no, it is useless to these insane follies they are the result of ignorance, or the vanity of ignorance, and proper physiological education, under the guidance of a moral sense, lofty and expansive with beauty, is the only prevention and cure.[10]

Already, the popular press was linking morality, purity, and self-determination with health and beauty. Even the trade press, like the *American Agriculturist*, decried the corrosive effects of commonly used beauty-industry ingredients, but instead of reform declared that "the best beautifiers are health, exercise, and good temper."[11]

The missive that was already being sold to women was that if you were not happy with your looks, that's on you—you're simply not working hard enough at it. This has long been an easy sell in a country born in religion, revolution, and free trade. White, Protestant, American popular culture has always fetishized the concept of "self-made." The thought being that with enough hard work, moxie, and discipline, a person could better his or her lot. It's a pure and lofty notion and one that works out for some but also one that conveniently ignores the extra hurdles long placed in the way of women, the poor, people of color, and everyone otherwise outside the mainstream model. This sky's-the-limit notion of prosperity was soon adapted to rigors of womanhood by removing the economic element and replacing it with the idea that good looks weren't just some genetic fluke, but something you controlled through virtuousness, modesty, and diligence.

Women's general-interest magazines, which offered wholesome amusements from embroidery patterns to sheet music, were often dotted with little dictums and satirical bits about avoiding makeup. *Port-Folio* offered, for example, a joke ad for "Dr. Moral's Celebrated Attracting Lip Salve," which supposedly consisted of "the genuine Gum Moderate, the essence of Kindness, dulcified Sugar of Gentleness, and Sweet Oil of Condescension."[†12] The *Guardian and Monitor* also had its own recipe, suggesting that the only "approved cosmetic" could be made as such: "To one full measure of piety, add ten grains recollection, also of conscious three scruples."[13] In addition to recommending moral rigor, the *Guardian and Monitor* was way ahead of the curve on the health and fitness craze, suggesting that in addition to a good dose of prayer, working out ("in the morning, before breakfast, a walk of a mile or more"[14]) and eating carefully could take the place of lipstick and powder.

The other ever-present element in who-can-wear-what is class. America, for all of its Enlightenment aspirations toward "liberty, fraternity, equality," has always trusted its rich, white, male citizens just a little bit more, as evidenced by those who first got the vote (i.e., white, male

---

† Note that they mean condescension in the early sense of the word, that is, to make gracious allowance, not being snooty. But I'm sure you knew that.

landowners). To some extent, this blind faith is extended to the wives and daughters of prosperous men of the upper class who were, therefore, allowed to play by their own set of rules when it came to makeup. For people who had the disposable income for style and society (or the inclination and price of a magazine to read about it), cosmetics seemed to be not an issue of moral fiber or hard work but one of fashion. In 1802, the year of Martha Washington's death, a nationally syndicated column breathlessly detailed the activities of the Washington, D.C., social season.

> Our belles are making the most spirited exertions for the ensuing campaign: hitherto, this season has been marked by gaiety, but this, it is intended, shall surpass in brilliance and elegance any that have been witnessed in the metropolis. . . . Corsets, stays, busks, puffs, paints, patches, powders, pastes, essences, rouge waters, etc., are all flowing in to us almost to inundation.[15]

Who appears tasteful in makeup and who appears deceptive was becoming increasingly attached to income level in the popular press. This warning was, of course, squarely aimed at women of the lower classes. You could risk it if you were not well-to-do, but nothing less than your free time and immortal soul were at stake. The *Boston Olive Branch* (a paper "devoted to Christianity, mutual rights, polite literature, general intelligence, agriculture, and the arts") editorialized about the dangers of emulating "The Belle," warning young ladies:

> What servitude to the toilette, what mixings, and patches, and cosmetics are applied, that the semblance of beauty may remain upon the faded temple—and what then of the soul, that deathless, mysterious engine of good or evil? . . . Oh! believe us young lady, you are far happier with a more moderate share of these perilous gifts, far more sure of a useful life, loving friends to gild your pathway, a peaceful death, a blissful hereafter, if you but strive to live purely and innocently in a world so filled with evil.[16]

In 1855, the year Cincinnati, Ohio, was burned in a riot between anti-immigration activists and German immigrants, *Graham's Monthly Magazine* editorialized that makeup on some women marked downward mobility, opining that

In all other countries the use of rouge is, excepting on the stage, entirely confined to a class whose morality and principles are as false as their complexions. In the United States, however, the use of both white powder and rouge is universal; and, in the South, used without any attempt at concealment. The ladies of New York begin their toilette by making up their faces—the ladies of Philadelphia do not so universally adopt this fashion.[17]

For women of the upper crust, makeup was simply a matter of personal flair and not morality.

Around the same time that the *Olive Branch* was warning the god-fearing women of Boston about damnation, the New York *Lantern* was praising the trendsetting style of the "Street Belle," who transcended class (but was also said to have been raised by a "French or English governess"):

The Street Belle is, perhaps, more important than any others in the corps of belles, because she is not confined to any particular class or rank of society, and may be considered as much a *femme elegante,* coming from below Bleeker, as if she made her exits and entrances from some stylish mansion about Fourteenth Street. . . . She is early taught to be an artist in colors, and uses her *blanc et rouge* with exquisite taste.[18]

Across various publications, the press seemed to suggest that this look was fine for the socialite who had the time and resources to become adept at cosmetic use and social graces but still a problem for the everyday American gal, who should continue to rely on grit and piety. Additionally, part of the problem from the point of view of anti-rouge critics actually may have been the training from that European nanny.

On top of the moral quandaries makeup presented to its detractors, painting represented foreignness and that simply wouldn't do for *real* Americans. From the very beginning in 1802, the second year of Jefferson's presidency, the *Port-Folio* winkingly prefaced its "Festoon of Fashion" column with the caveat, "As it is notorious that American women neither paint their cheeks, nor 'daub their tempers o'er with washes as artificial as their faces,' we publish the following merely as a satire of *European* deception. We do not dream that any *Domestic* application can be made."[19] Emphasis theirs. The sneer likely was rooted in the notion that we hadn't just liberated ourselves from the Crown so that our women could prance around like a bunch of highfalutin courtiers. We were Americans now and we had to set some guidelines about what that meant in terms of social norms and modes of dress around here. *The Lady's Book* was downright angry about the thought of makeup trends possibly being imported from Britain; an editorial huffed at the utter gall of a contemporary article suggesting otherwise, "*The Albany Daily Advertiser* says, 'An English writer charges fashionable females who ruin their health and their complexions by their dissipation with resorting to many artifices to retain their good looks'. . . . Such may be the case in England but can never be here."[20] You hear that? Cosmetics are both bad for your health *and* foreign.

By the mid-nineteenth century, our global influence growing, immigration ticking up, our borders staggering West, and tensions growing over slavery within them, who and what constituted American-ness became a serious question to a great many citizens. As with many forms of patriotism, these definitions both united the nation by providing a defined sense of belonging and divided it by giving members of any self-proclaimed in-group a quick shorthand to identify and exclude "others."

For the Whig Party of that period, keeping America for supposed Americans was at the core of everything it did. We hadn't existed as a nation for a full century and already the Whigs were trying to make it great again. One particularly impassioned letter to the editor of the Whig paper, the *Louisville Morning Courier*, suggested that American women should again reject the foreign influence of fashion in favor of what was dubbed "true Americanism." Hearkening back to the patriotic women of the Revolution who had forgone imports of domestic items for the war effort, the writer suggested that "they doubtless looked as lovely in their homespun gowns, their eyes lighted with the fires of liberty, their cheeks flushed with the glow of patriotism, and the health-blood of domestic industry" as opposed to the "finished belle of the current day, in full Parisian costume—her eyebrows arched with black lead and her cheeks blushed with the slightest tinge of pokeberry juice . . . or even the most approved, imported 'vegetable rouge.'"[21] Nationalism could now be added to the growing list of virtues that brought out your eyes as well as any cosmetic.

Somewhere between the Continental Congress and Fort Sumter, America had found its voice, or, more accurately, a number of raucous, competing voices with a range of ideas about what it meant to be lady-like, healthy, stylish, pious, honest, marriageable, ambitious, and even

American. "As nothing is more flattering than the art of preserving beauty and adorning the exterior of our persons, it is not surprising that the use of cosmetics is one of the most universal practices of civilized nations."[22] Makeup was political, it was financial, it was civilization and science. The coming decades would lead to even more debate around lipstick wearing as the nation grappled with the notions about women and their place in abolition, temperance, suffrage, industrialization, immigration, migration, evangelism, and more. When it came to women and their toilet,[‡] however, the stage was set; beauty would be a matter of public interest and one that bore the weight of all fears, joys, and ambitions.

---

‡ Still funny.

CHAPTER TWO

THE ROUGE BADGE OF COURAGE
The Civil War to the Twentieth Century

Shade of the Decade
Velontine's Indelible Natural Tint Rouge

B y 1861 our fragile, neophyte union had grown to include thirty-three states—each with a lot on their mind. With every corner of the nation struggling internally with how best to handle the serious issues of the day ranging from slavery to industrialization to westward expansion to immigration to the most efficient way to contact the dead, America was on the fast track to becoming a major player in the modern world via stops and switches through the exacting mores, strange fads, and baroque preoccupations of the Victorian era. All of the young nation's concerns would be thrown into sharp focus, of course, on April 12 of that year, when the starting guns of the Civil War sounded across the parapets of Fort Sumter. Over the course of four short years, the new nation would be torn in two and bound together again, emerging on the other side as a nation of considerable consumer strength, religious fervor, and now familiar social themes.

Named for Her Majesty Victoria (by the grace of God, of the United Kingdom of Great Britain and Ireland queen, defender of the faith, empress of India), the era is most remembered for its straitlaced sensibilities and fascination with death and mourning. Timely and understandable, given the amount of loss the average citizen faced during a lifetime due to disease, war, and a generally hardscrabble existence; morbidity was an aesthetic that expressed itself on both sides of the Atlantic in everything from fashion to architecture. In terms of beauty, the ideal itself was placed squarely at death's door and tied up in black ribbons. Pallor led the list of must-haves for the fashionable girl, so much so that in addition to gloves, hats, and parasols to prevent any exposure to the dreaded sun, some women washed with ammonia, ingested arsenic-laced wafers, and endured a makeup process known as enameling for that just-went-to-her-great-reward glow. Enameling was pretty much what it sounded like; the process involved makeup artists painting the skin with an "enamel" mixture of white lead paste and other ingredients, thereby obliterating any freckles, dark spots, or flaws. For added realism, blue veins were drawn in, as well. The results might be flawless, but they were also toxic and fragile, so anyone wearing it was encouraged to stand still without expressing any big emotion, lest her face literally crack. John Singer Sargent's 1884 *Portrait of Madame X* captures the process at its height on the socialite Virginie Gautreau, who stands poised and aloof, her waist corseted into eccentric curves and her exposed skin gleaming like marble—the Gilded Age captured in paint. High maintenance and totally impractical for anyone who had to do chores, care for a child, or any other menial tasks without the aid of servants, the look whispers of money and privilege.

Although it was the height of fashion, it was also the butt of jokes. In May 1862 as General Thomas J. "Stonewall" Jackson implemented his campaign against the North in the Shenandoah Valley, the *Saturday Evening Post* compared the look to the new battleships of the Union and the Confederacy.

> The face is covered with a complete enamel and is said to present an appearance the peculiar character of which can be recognized at once. . . . In these days of iron-clads, it is perhaps only consistent that the ladies' figureheads should be porcelain-clad. And the latter we should think would be as impervious to the soft artillery of Cupid, winged rosy from the lips, as the former from the more destructive bolts of Armstrongs and Dahlgrens.*[1]

---

* Naval artillery, specifically large-bore cannons.

The look was not topped off with a bright lip. Maybe a pale wash of color, but nothing livelier than that. That's not to say the use of lip rouge disappeared during this period. More likely, it went underground; modesty about all personal matters and the perceived boundaries of gender were central obsessions of the era. Again, depending on your income level and moral compass, you might powder or pomade a bit before you left your home, but you certainly didn't tell people about it anymore than you would discuss the intimacies of hiking up your pantaloons or squeezing into your stays. You were simply assumed to have rolled out of bed with a wasp waist and a ghostly glow and no one had to know otherwise. Talking about the details of fashion was vanity, and vanity was the weakness of women—mainly.

Drag and other forms of female impersonation[†] likely has existed for most of human history, emerging just seconds after whatever moment in time that agreed-upon gender norms were established. Nineteenth-century Europe and America, having abandoned the unisex rouge and powder of the eighteenth century, had a huge stake in letting everyone know exactly what the rules were due to their predominant, unbending concept of male and female spheres in all aspects of life and work. So if makeup was considered devious on a woman, you can imagine the fuss if it was found on a man. Though not exactly drag in the theatrical sense, in 1862 one Charles Walter made front-page news in Boston (after leaving behind troubles in New York, Baltimore, and Washington, D.C.) for appearing as the "Lady in Black." Charles's scam wasn't overly complicated; she or he (pronoun preference unknown) posed as a vulnerable widow, flirted with soldiers, and soon thereafter extracted cash in exchange for promises of love, going so far as to become engaged to a man in Baltimore. Which, the *Boston Herald* seemed to think was an understandable mistake on the part of the fiancé, since "In appearance [Charles] is womanish, beardless, with long black curling hair, and by the aid of rouge and cosmetics makes a very deceptive individual."[2] These assumptions gave beauty products both enormous power and made their supposed misuse incredibly dangerous to the red-blooded American male.

The rules of gender were being established for decades to come. The emerging narrative largely held that female vanity was silly, but it was

---

† That is, performative gender, not gender identity or expression.

part of the job of being a woman and practically genetic; male vanity was a downright abomination. Youth and manly vigor were already the standard. As the *San Francisco Examiner* explained, "Of all fops in existence, the old fop is the most contemptible . . . who is scented and perfumed . . . who uses dyes and cosmetics that the marks of age may be obliterated, and the bloom of youth imitated."[3] Any relationship between men and color cosmetics was to be hidden for generations to come; for women, it would be tolerated but closely monitored for excess and moral decay. "Fashion," declared contemporary lecturer, countess, and muse, Lola Montez,[‡] "began its sway in the Garden of Eden and originated in the follies and sins of mankind. . . . The only rouge they used was the natural bloom, and dyes and colors were creation of a later date to spell the pure beauty of Eve's daughters."[4]

The war between the states would end with General Robert E. Lee's surrender at Appomattox in April 1865, but the now United States would continue to battle for hearts and minds when it came to beauty and artifice. Thinking beyond the South's stated reasons for secession and the victory of the Union, it's hard to overstate the impact that the Civil War and the following Reconstruction would have on the culture, industry, and the makeup of America for the years to come. In the decades after the war, there would occur seismic shifts in population from rural to urban; commerce from agriculture to manufacturing; and vast wealth created for a sliver of the population. Further, with the hard-won goal of abolition achieved, reform-minded Americans were now freed up to pursue some of their other passions, including (but not limited to): health crazes, pseudo-sciences, temperance, evangelism, spiritualism, and suffrage. All of which would intersect with each other and the burgeoning cosmetic industry in some way soon enough.

Health and its implications in particular would become a major topic of public conversation. The natural corollary of the death fixation, the focus on diet, exercise, and other clean-living activities offered a measure of perceived control in a world that was still learning about germ theory and

---

‡ Born Eliza Rosanna Gilbert in County Limerick, Ireland, Mme. Montez was granted her authority on fashion by virtue of having been a celebrated (and scandalous) "Spanish dancer" on the Continent as well as courtesan to King Ludwig I of Bavaria, mistress to composer Franz Liszt, and friend to author George Sand. She's also said to be the inspiration for Sherlock Holmes's foil Irene Adler, who was featured in "A Scandal in Bohemia."

anesthesia. Although some health "experts" stuck with plain instruction, many regimens emerged with a sincerely American layer of moralizing and aspiration.

In 1868, shortly before the country's first presidential impeachment trial of Andrew Johnson, the *Christian Advocate* opposed the use of makeup on moral grounds, though it didn't hurt its argument that science was on its side. "To heighten their beauty in the eyes of admiring gentlemen, the ladies are resorting to various cosmetics in the shape of washes, powders, and paints, which are put up and lauded to the skies by greedy and unprincipled knaves calling themselves druggists, as sovereign remedies for all the evils which beset a fair complexion." Adding the ominous warning, "Now the ladies ought to know that all preparations are more or less injurious to the skin when used habitually, and some of them poisonous, and dangerous to health and life."[5] It sounds dire, but again with no government regulation and lead as a top ingredient in most formulas, there probably was an element of truth to the scare tactics that made vanity a literal deadly sin.

The religious press was hardly alone in its condemnation of adornment. Even the more esoteric interests also validated the perspective that women risking their health for beauty was both dangerous and degenerate. *Eclectic Magazine of Foreign Literature* insisted that "A lady about to paint, or varnish, or enamel herself, has first, if she be wise, to consider the matter from a hygienic or health-disposing point of view."[6] Although, for lip color's sake (and following in Martha Washington's footsteps), it conceded that "Roseate pomades are never, on account of their coloring-matter, objectionable, the tint being imparted by alkanet root, which is wholly innocuous."[7] *Albion: A Journal of News, Politics and Literature*[§] warned of the hollowness and degeneration of the "Fashionable Woman," lamenting that "she will not try simplicity of living, natural hours, wholesome occupation, unselfish endeavor, but rushes off for help to paints and cosmetics, to stimulants and drugs, and attempts to restore the faded freshness of her beauty by the very means which further corrode it."[8]

[§] The *Albion* was a well-regarded literary magazine of the era, which boasted (among other things) the first publication of Charles Dickens in America and one of the few contemporary reviews of Walt Whitman's then avant-garde poetry collection, *Leaves of Grass*. Sadly, it was also one of Whitman's only positive notices, largely due to the fact that he wrote it himself anonymously.

Additionally, it wasn't only the cosmopolitan press of the East Coast that concerned itself with the perilous effects of makeup. By this time, opportunities that arose due to the Homestead Act, the Gold Rush, and the construction of a transcontinental railway had drawn the adventurous (and the truly broke) westward, creating new towns and cities along the way. Because it was a frontier and most migrants went in search of jobs or economic opportunity, men often ventured ahead alone, either as bachelors or married men who sent for wives and children later, skewing the population by as much as 20 percent in favor of men. An 1874 map,[9] for example, shows majority male populations concentrated at the borders of the Indian Territories and other uncolonized frontier lands. This meant fewer women, but obviously not no women; those who did strike out to the lands west of the Mississippi did so as homesteaders, sex workers, missionaries, teachers, domestics, and all of the other limited options open to women.

It's here that our collective imagination splits somewhat from the historical record. Americans, being largely enamored of pop culture, sometimes cast fictional characters in important roles in our collective memory of actual history. For the West (and the era, in general), it's the idea of the "painted lady" versus the wholesome pioneer wife or schoolmarm. Although there's probably an element of truth to the idea that some saloon girls, brothel workers, and entertainers painted and good girls didn't, it later became embedded in our collective consciousness by Hollywood characters—such as *Gone with the Wind*'s madame, Belle Watling, *Gunsmoke*'s saloon owner, Miss Kitty, the smoky-eyed "fembots" of *Westworld*, and so on—rather than the actual day-to-day lives of these women. Articles in the local newspapers suggest that women in general had the same level of interest in and concerns about makeup as their counterparts "back East."

How the local press handled makeup varied from sparkling coverage about the curiosities of fashion to complaints about safety. In Nebraska, "making up" was written off as impractical, and women were advised that the fashionable ladies of Paris found that "The scarlet lip salves, which are sometimes employed, come off too easily, and have, besides a tendency to run, which is destructive to all appearances of reality."[10] Chickasaw County, Iowa, on the other hand, featured the consumer fantasy of one Paris atelier and its enormous range of colors ("over a dozen different shades of rouge") and lip colors, which were the "finest and most artistic make-up of all, and also the costliest."[11] Conversely, in Tin Cup, Colorado, women were warned off "Poisonous Face Powders," although a St. Louis doctor quoted in the article approved lip balm, since "It has strong adhesive properties, but is probably non-poisonous."[12]

Not that all of the new West was mining towns and farmland. San Francisco, which was already on its way to becoming a major metropolis on par with New York and Chicago, touted the California lifestyle as a good substitute for cosmetics, with the *Chronicle* proposing in 1883 (the year that the Brooklyn Bridge opened to traffic) that "we fancy that San Francisco women are physically superior to their sisters in the Eastern States. A more congenial climate, with the advantage for outdoor walks nearly every day in the year is the chief cause of the superiority." But even so, it lamented the influence of fashion trends reaching west of the Rockies, adding a racist and puritanical flourish regarding the use of eye makeup and lip color: "American men, as a rule, do not like the slavish imitation of Oriental customs. In a harem of [Istanbul], the penciling of eyebrow, the rouging of cheek, the painting of lips—all of these adornments which have become second nature in the Far East—are appropriate."[13] Again, makeup was not only foreign, but corrupting and impure to the fresh-faced California girls of song and legend.

Despite the West's diversity from the beginning, women of color would be largely left out of the mainstream conversation around beauty consumption for years to come. In America, born of the original sin of slavery and xenophobia, racism and beauty would intersect in more ways than one. Phrenology, for example—a wildly popular nineteenth-century discipline that maintained that character traits and human potential could be "read" by its practitioners through an expert prodding of the bumps on the skull—suggested that women wanting to be beautiful could move beyond the limits of their given noggins through healthy living, deep breathing, and piety. White women, anyway. The study of cranial lumps of the skulls of people of color indicated that they were somehow a lower order of being and lacking potential. Although the practice would fade from popular culture as the century wore on, it first would provide a so-called scientific rationale to white supremacy that would take other forms (such as eugenics) later on.

The *American Phrenological Journal* told readers "How to Be Beautiful," though it was a rather tall order.

> You must, if you do not already possess it, acquire good health. Without this there can be no complete and satisfactory personal attractiveness. . . . There must be a good digestion to nourish and give proper fullness to the frame; an active circulation to convey the nutritive particles to every part and carry off the effete matter from the system; good lungs and full breathing to oxygenize and thereby vitalize the blood (for it is blood that glows on the lip and blushes on the cheek), in short, there must be complete organic and functional integrity.[14]

Cosmetics would not help create a "sublime altitude to the coronal arch of the cranium,"[15] only hard work and good breeding could do that. No matter how wacky the basis, it was one more outlet insisting that resorting to lip color was somehow a moral failing on the part of women.

On the political spectrum, the call for women's suffrage was gaining momentum and launching a new public conversation on what it meant to be a woman in a country that was speeding toward a bright, new future of prosperity and modernity. Lipstick—at this point, anyway—didn't seem to have much of a place in this movement. Between the stated goals of securing the vote and acquiring some basic human rights for the "weaker sex," there were bigger fish for suffragists to fry in the closing years of the nineteenth century. However, Elizabeth Cady Stanton¶ did mention that she viewed women's clothing specifically as both mentally and physically hobbling. In 1870, she offered a now familiar refrain to a St. Louis audience: "Our fashions are sent to us . . . by French courtezans [*sic*]." She also noted that cosmetics were poisonous and subscribed to the notion that plenty of fresh air and exercise "would beautify the complexion and did not cost 75-cents a bottle."[16] Though her objections seem more practical than polemical (and very on trend for their time), they did mark the beginnings of the complicated and often contentious relationship that various generations of feminists would have with makeup.

¶ Born to a prosperous family in New York State 1815, Stanton would devote most of her eighty-six years to fighting for women's rights. In 1848, she was the principal author of the Declaration of Sentiments, which was modeled on the Declaration of Independence and first outlined the demands of the women's movement in America.

While American women would wait another half-century for the vote, within a decade the conversation around makeup would begin to shift dramatically; slowly at first, but changes were definitely coming. Stumbling blocks would be recast as stepping-stones with the negative associations around lipstick being recast as assets that could offer wearers the trappings of health, upward mobility, and modernity. The rise of advertising and mass media also played a major role in the evolving makeover. With a growing number of magazines, newspapers, books, and pamphlets available to the public, it was easier to learn about the newest and greatest things with unprecedented speed. This was especially important with vast influx of western and southern European immigrants, who along with the expansion of the U.S. territory led to a 26 percent jump[17] in the population, and a whole new segment of consumers and citizens who had to be instructed on what it was to live like an American.

Additionally, more and faster access to information meant that it was possible to become famous with greater ease. Celebrity, as we currently understand it, is a relatively modern invention and one that requires a

The original influencer. Lillian Russell was among the first celebrities to endorse a line of cosmetics. *NYPL Collection*

reliable means of spreading information widely in a short amount of time. The rise of the daily press in America meant that fame was no longer the space of royalty and politicians; humbly born entertainers, authors, and other notable folks now had a shot at notoriety, if not eternity. Daily papers (and later radio, film, TV, and the internet) meant a greater number of everyday people were becoming household names, and their daily exploits could be followed by an entertainment-hungry public.

If there was a Victorian equivalent of the modern-day influencer, Lillian Russell was it. Born on December 4, 1861, as Helen Louise Leonard in Clinton, Iowa, she rose to fame singing light opera and was soon dubbed the "American Beauty" for her bubbly persona, flawless complexion, and tight-laced curves. From her first theatrical triumph in 1881 to her death in 1912, reporters breathlessly covered everything from her husbands (four of them), her boyfriends (most notably, financier and playboy "Diamond Jim" Brady), her then outré exercise routine (bicycling without a corset), and her lavish fashions (those involved corsets). She also may have been one of the first celebrities to formally endorse a brand of cosmetics.

In 1885, newspapers up and down the East Coast reported her absence from a performance of her hit Broadway show. "At the opening of last evening's performance of 'Polly' at the Casino it was announced that Miss Lillian Russell was unable to appear. A certificate, signed by her physician, was read. According to this her face was so badly swollen from the effects from the use of cosmetics that it was not advisable for her to sing that evening."[18] A minor setback and hardly a surprise given the toxic contents of most colorants and treatments, she (or her management) may have sensed an opportunity in her injury, as several months later in the Business Points column, it was announced she was lending her name to a Detroit-based beauty concern.

> Referring to theatrical plays, we desire to say that Minnie Palmer, Lillian Russell, and other actresses of fame and beauty, have given the proprietors of "Parfumerie Monte Christo" to refer to them as to the great merits of Eugenie's Secrets of Beauty as a great purifier and beautifier for the complexion; also, Velontine Face Powders and Indelible Natural Tint Rouges.[19]

Though it was no secret that theater performers painted and their reputations were still somewhat suspect, here was a much-admired operetta singer sharing her beauty secrets with the sort of respectable, middle- or working-class ladies who read the morning paper. Why shouldn't she too enjoy the male admiration that came along with purified skin and natural rouges? It was perhaps a small step toward legitimacy with a select clientele but one that the beauty industry would continue to rely on all the way into the current Instagram era.

More women could be convinced of the benefits of buying into beauty—advertisers and columnists would increasingly stake their reputations on it—but it would take some doing. Makeup was clearly a phenomenon that was here to stay, although the stigma of wearing color still clung to women. The *Daily American* interviewed one drugstore clerk who supposed that "You will probably not find one woman out of a thousand who does not use some sort of face powder." The clerk added that "It is different with paint. More women use paint now than in the history of the world. . . . Yet they are alike about buying. They do not want anyone to see them make a purchase or to know that they have such a thing among their toilet articles." The key to overcoming that reticence was to adapt the messaging to subtly address the concerns raised over the years. Part of selling this new, pro-makeup agenda would rely on creating a new class of experts. People who claimed intimate knowledge of the various available preparations and solutions and could steer women clear of the pitfalls into which others had foolishly wandered. It also expanded beauty's borders beyond the local druggist's counters to something aspirational and reimagined cosmetics as a tasteful, feminine luxury item rather than something picked up at the same place you would purchase diaper rash ointment, patent medicine, and ice cream sodas. Not that drugstore makeup was going anywhere, but makeup reenvisioned as a luxury item enhanced its sophistication and intensified one's desire to acquire it.

Local ads throughout the country claimed their beauty parlors offered "A Professor of Physical and Esthetic Culture and the High Art of Beauty"[20] or a "Thoroughly Competent Beauty Doctor."[21] Another popular self-granted title was simply "Madame," such as Madame Ruppert, who said she was "New York's leading complexion expert" and democratically claimed that "Beauty can be made as well as born."[22] This *nom de beauté* was a particularly great option for female operators, since it imparted the practitioner with a posh foreign air and cashed in on the idea that the French possessed advanced understanding of beauty (without the hassle of having to acquire an actual degree). It was so convincing an affectation that it actually persisted well into the twentieth century for big names such as Mme. Helena Rubinstein.

Although there was a growing number of professionals studying what would come to be known as "beauty culture," this was, of course, an era before vigorous licensing requirements and agreed-upon curriculums. So nothing really stopped ambitious entrepreneurs from declaring themselves experts and hanging a shingle, a custom that would soon prove both dangerous and pioneering by creating a whole new generation of beauty culturists with grand ambitions and some formidable business sense.

On the editorial side, writers were adopting a new voice that relied less on principled scolding and more on friendly advice given by yet another set of experts. For this segment, simply having a byline was considered enough to constitute expertise. Some recommended hot baths as the best thing for the complexion, some swore by cold baths; nearly all agreed that proper eating and brisk walking was the secret to youth and beauty. With very little formal research and few experts, every guess was pretty much as good as the next. When it came to makeup, some authors still warned that ingredients alone prohibited use, whereas others were beginning to see ways that cosmetics could work for some. The *Chicago Tribune* revealed some of the secrets of society girls' "Toilet Mysteries"** to its readers under the subhead that "Soap and Face Powders Are Useful When Handled Properly—A Few Hints."[23] The *Philadelphia Inquirer* viewed making up as a trend to which all women would eventually succumb, so the smart girl might as well make the best of it, stating that "if you have made up your mind that a dash of color will improve your sallow skin, select your rouge with care. A cheap article will likely be filled with vermillion, which will undoubtedly ruin the skin."[24]

Additionally, between the fashion pages and beauty practitioners, a layer of xenophobia was being stripped away in one very specific area: you now could turn to the French as trustworthy sources of information on how to select and use color cosmetics. In New Orleans, the *Times-Picayune* declared that "French women know better than those of any

---

** Still funny.

other nation about the subtleties of cosmetics, and the art which conceals art is what is aimed for by the Parisienne, be she grisette†† or grand dame."[25] While *Hall's Journal of Health* haled "The Way Women Bathe in Paris," particularly the way they put themselves back together after a refreshing dip in the Seine, "On leaving the baths, they dry their hair sufficiently, put a crimped [wig] over their own straight locks, a dash of powder, and a bit of lip salve (a stick of which every French woman carries in her pocket) to slightly color and avoid any dryness."[26]

Although none of these constitutes a ringing endorsement by the modern press, makeup was being acknowledged as something women wanted and the conversation was evolving. More accurately put: attitudes surrounding makeup was changing for women—and women only. Men wearing cosmetics would continue to be seen as a violation of some unwritten but widely known subclause of the social contract. It was an area of great concern for much of the media, which viewed it with a jaundiced curiosity about whether it took the form of self-expression or vanity. In this area of use, secrecy was infinitely important, more so than with women who wanted to avoid the run-of-the-mill tutting about vanity.

"The practice of painting and powdering the faces of young men is very much more common than anyone acquainted with the tricks of the gilt-edged youths of Cleveland would imagine," dished one drugstore clerk. Adding that men wished to hide the effects of hard work and hard partying, "Then in an evil hour some effeminate conceived the startling idea of burying these facial defects beneath cosmetic compounds."[27] No secret was safe in Ohio, as not two years later a professional makeup artist revealed that she had been painting the men of Cincinnati. Primping them with rouge and pencils, she confessed, "I could tell you the names of a dozen young men whose faces I prepared for an evening's entertainment last week and they were not all dudes either." In this context, *dudes* means "dandies" or effeminate, fashionable men. Shortened from "doodle," as in Yankee Doodle Dandy. However, she demurred when it came to naming names, confessing that "I guess I have told you too much already."[28] There was no client-druggist privilege in Boston, either, with a clerk revealing, "It's sad to see how men use cosmetics. They seem to care more about looking pretty than schoolgirls do. Why, even the girls themselves

---

†† A working-class woman.

get ashamed of it and declare they are disgusted, and will depend upon long walks, cold water, and flannel for their complexions and stop using powder of any kind."[29]

While the newspapers were shaking down clerks for information about how men were sneaking powder and paint, women were increasingly turning to more niche media—the woman's magazine. These magazines were aimed at women's domestic interests, offering everything from short romance stories to chicken recipes and laundry hints. They were designed to present an idealized and yet somehow achievable vision of the happy home. Ranging in subject matter from the middle-class domestic arts of housekeeping and childrearing to the more privileged pursuits of society such as dressing appropriately for the social whirl of occasions such as travel and theater, these magazines would come to be a central source of information for many socially ambitious women. Whether they were new citizens looking to learn the subtleties and expectations of what it was to be an ideal American or middle-class housewives browsing the lifestyles of the rich and famous as a form of aspiration, in the years to come these outlets would increasingly control the conversation around makeup and its proper use—that is, as soon as they figured out how they felt about it.

In 1884, as the last bricks were added to the Washington Monument, *Harper's Bazaar* acknowledged the complicated nature and its mixed feelings about the responsibilities of caring for the "Modern Complexions":

> The "people of the theatre" have thoroughly learned how to use their cosmetics but the ladies of leisure and fashion are so ignorant of the *science* of the care of the complexion that cases where the skin is completely ruined are of everyday occurrence and it seems impossible to credit that only forty years ago a sign of fine lady-ism or good breeding was a fresh *natural* complexion.[30]

The ladies' press would be only too glad to tell these women the formulas needed to maintain their skin's health so they could continue making up, thereby establishing their columns on beauty as both an authority and friend.

Conversely, *Good Housekeeping* was still skeptical that makeup was the proper thing for its audience of respectable, flag-waving, middle-class wives and mothers. It established its authority in another way, clucking in the article "Touching the Toilet"‡‡ that "if it be allowable to refer to the complexion and the use of cosmetics and powders, let the opportunity be taken to utter one earnest protest against the cruel habit or fashion of which is ruining so many of our American faces."[31] The magazine would, of course, change its tune in the years to come, but it's important to note that *Good Housekeeping* (and in the twentieth century, its branded *Good Housekeeping Seal* for consumers) was a primer of sorts for thousands of women navigating an unfamiliar modern world and its demands. Whether new to the country, relocated from farms to cities, or the first generation to find themselves in the middle class, women of the late nineteenth century would face issues that their mothers and grandmothers hadn't even considered, such as how to answer the telephone or guide children through public dating. This and many other household magazines would help create the middle class and reinforce their sense of propriety in a way that can't be overstated.

In the formation of modern America, 1892 would prove to be an eventful year: Ellis Island began accepting immigrants, Thomas Edison patented the two-way telegraph, and women got their first copies of *Vogue*. *Vogue* would be the ne plus ultra in fashion and beauty coverage for a well-heeled, savvy segment of population—eventually. At the beginning, it too did not see the charm of the painted face but was ready to accept its inevitability. In instructing readers "How to Be Beautiful," the Marquise de Panhael begrudgingly gave some tips on balancing one's look with her complexion.

> I have heard actresses, whose profession obliges them to have recourse *maquillage*, loudly deplore its effects on their complexions, and it is, therefore, a mystery to me why women of the world who have no need to do so insist on plastering their skin with all sorts of pastes and powders, which to begin with deceive nobody and, which I may safely add, give any woman an appearance of doubtful respectability.
>
> But enough preaching, and let us come to the point, for I know that my admonitions are without avail, and that in spite of it all, society belles will continue to "make up" as if I had abstained from any warning from that direction. "*Qui a bu, boira*" ["who once drank will drink"], says the

---

‡‡ Okay, last one for a while. Go ahead and enjoy it.

French proverb, to which I feel inclined to add "Qui s'est maquillé, se maquillera" ["who has once made up will continue to make up"].[32]

The Marquise wasn't wrong in her complaints about cosmetics' effects and reputation, but she was chic—in the original sense of "smart"—to see what was coming. By 1900 *Vogue* would tone down its tsk-tsking and start to talk about makeup as a secret among women, admitting that part of shopping included browsing for lip colors: "It need only be hinted that among the thousand and one other articles I examined were the latest and most approved rouges, powders, eye and lip crayons."[33]

In the following years, women would set their own rules about wanting and needing lipstick and other cosmetics, but as the nineteenth century drew to a close, the foundation was laid. Technology would change formulas, economic growth would make an industry possible, and even how and when women were seen in public would create the conditions necessary for the imminent phenomena. Race, class, gender, capitalism, and patriotism would all add their voices to the conversation, but the lipstick century was coming, and America would lead the way.

CHAPTER THREE

SPEAK SOFTLY AND CARRY A LIP STICK
1900–1918

Shades of the Decade
Lillian Russell My Own Lip Rouge
Rigaud's Mary Garden Lip Stick
Palmolive Lip Rouge
Madame Yale's Jack Rose Bud Lip Tint
Cherryola Grease Rouge for Lips or Cheeks

For America, the excitement around entering the twentieth century was positively electric. Despite a civil war, Reconstruction, several panics, a handful of recessions, and some ill-advised skirmishes at home and abroad, we emerged from the late nineteenth century as a force to be reckoned with militarily, technologically, financially, and culturally. We invented the phone, the light bulb, the steam engine, the roller coaster, and bubble gum—surely there was no limit to what we could achieve. With the possibilities wide open, the nation's eyes were fixed on the future and the bright promise of the modern world.

Women (who were still fighting for suffrage and the most basic of property rights) could take heart, because that optimism included the beauty world. "The century just dawned is brimming with wonders," marveled the *Philadelphia Inquirer*. Adding that "Perhaps you don't know, my dear mademoiselle, that the best modern rouge is as great an improvement on grease paint as Marconi's wireless telegraphy is on an improvement on the ancient post boy."[1]

Moreover, as if to put a point on the eponymous era, Queen Victoria died on January 22, 1901, just three weeks after the new century was rung in. Although not exactly earthshaking for Americans, it allowed for a change in attitudes about cosmetics in high society and the press—which actually had been coming for a while—to get going in earnest. The American papers noted with some glee "Alexandra's Approval of Rouge."

> Endorsed by Queen Alexandra, rouge is now used as openly in England nowadays as in the unregenerate days of Louis XV. After the wicked French days paint fell into discredit and Victorian respectability placed a ban on rouge. Thus, tabooed it remained in disrespect until revived by Queen Alexandra, who controls the fashion authoritatively.[2]

This was relevant to the women of America, because their own version of aristocracy (i.e., the very rich) also was adopting the practice quickly: "Eight women in ten in New York society paint. . . . Every hostess has a lip stick or pot of rouge in the dressing room at her entertainments."[3]

As a neologism, lip stick was two words but just the fact of its existence was a novelty and proof that its star was on the rise. At this juncture even small technological, economic, and social changes would culminate in major transformations. In 1900, for example, America was a country of approximately 75,995,000[4] people. The who, where, and what of that population was changing both drastically and quickly, rising more than 9 percent from 1895, due mainly to an influx of Western European immigrants;[5] the transition from majority rural to majority urban in a single generation;[6] and an increasing number of women employed outside the home in nonagricultural jobs.[7] This meant more women than ever were out in public spaces, had a certain measure of buying power, and access to a wider range of manufactured goods, all of which created the perfect atmosphere for a pocket-sized beauty item to thrive. That is, if carrying it in your pocket was a viable option. Lip stick, now in a more recognizable shape, was sold as a crayonlike product wrapped in wax paper and placed in a cardboard box but not yet in a metal tube, so it's still a bit of a mess for the busy gal on the go. Getting it into a convenient, portable form would be crucial to its success.

For reasons of both modesty and practicality, lip color was largely a vanity table item for most of its history. Wax or grease based, it melted if it got too warm, spilling in pockets and purses and permanently staining everything it touched. Before the patented push-up tube (stay tuned, that's coming soon), entrepreneurs tried several portable forms with varying degrees of success. One particularly popular way was to disguise lip rouges, salves, and pencils as jewelry, thereby preserving the secret. In some ways this is not unlike the advent of the earliest TV sets of the 1950s, which were huge, hulking objects encased in simulated wood-grain cabinets to give them a more furniture-like feel, because sometimes the easiest way to get consumers to accept a new item is to hide it within an already familiar form.

In 1900, the *Boston Daily Globe* marveled that

> The newest wrinkle the up-to-date girl has raised to the dignity of a fad is a small gold ball swinging from her bracelet on a slender chain. It looks like it were an ornament or some new kind of Oriental bangle, but in reality it is a hollow case with a sliding spring that opens the sphere, disclosing a rose-hued paste which the wearer describes as "lip salve." . . . The modern girl has been carrying a tiny powder puff and her mirror on her chatelaine* for several seasons, but lip salve on her bracelet chain is an entirely new and novel idea from Eastern harems by way of Paris.[8]

Available at multiple price points, these accessory items democratized carrying lipstick by making them available to women at a number of income levels. In Pittsburgh, they were advertised by the Joseph Horne Co., which proffered that "Mi'Lady's 'Vanity' May Be as Complete as She May Desire," asking women to indulge in a bit of consumer fantasy by building the custom chatelaine of their dreams. "Suppose when you are shopping a memorandum is desired. A memorandum tablet is handy; and alongside and jingling with it may be a coin purse, a mirror, a powder box, a hairpin holder, possibly a 'lip stick.'"[9]

Lipstick technology was also evolving along with other inventions that made it necessary to reconsider the old ways of painting at home, simply because women—especially young women—were simply out of

---

* A note on the chatelaine: bags and pockets for women have gone in and out of fashion over the centuries for reasons that range from misogyny to manufacturing; in their absence, women of the Victorian and Edwardian eras often carried small, everyday items such as scissors, notebooks, keys, thimbles, and so forth on a chain attached to their belts or pinned to their bodice.

the house more. Take the car, for example: according to the Federal Highway Administration in 1900, there were 8,000 cars registered in the United States; in 1910 it was 468,500.[10] In Charleston, the papers noted the impact the car was having on fashion.

> There is a positive mania for little vanity articles that may be carried in a shopping bag or pocket, and manufacturers are meeting the demand heroically. Fresh interest in such things is due to the prevalence of disheveling motoring and there are the most complete of motor bags containing in a small and compact form all the toilet accessories that could be needed after a motor spin.[11]

Along with the internal combustion engine, Americans had developed a taste for speed (such as it was—Ford's Model T topped out at about 40 miles per hour) and everything that could be, would be made "to go."

Besides joyriding, more women—although by no means a majority— were working outside of the house in factory jobs and in the domains that would come to define pink-collar careers (e.g., teacher, clerk, nurse, waitress, etc.). Among them was a new class of service professionals dedicated to "beauty culture," which was the idea that personal attractiveness could be cultivated through hairdressing, manicures, facials, and so on with the help of knowledgeable specialists. The notion rests comfortably within the idea that in America, you can always better your lot. This was particularly poignant in an era in which stock speculators and inventors created vast wealth for themselves. If women knew they were largely excluded from boardrooms, offices, and labs, they also would come to understand that beauty was its own form of currency, literally and figuratively.

For everyone from counter girls to beauticians to entrepreneurs, the beauty industry would provide jobs and opportunities for women, particularly marginalized women, when other male-dominated industries firmly shut their doors. It offered opportunity for a few during the years in which it was near impossible for women to raise capital and a particularly successful venture for those who were able to find a new angle or hustle on consumer demand. In 1902, the year that the first movie theater opened in Los Angeles, the *San Francisco Chronicle* was surprised to find a woman turning her skill into a living.

> Here is the most unique and original occupation for women that has yet been added to the list of feminine professions. In fact, the clever young woman who discovered the field prefers to call it an art rather than a profession. Whatever the name, this is the occupation: teaching society women to make up. . . . Miss Francis Hamilton is the high priestess of this "found art," and behind the skillful wielding of the lip stick and rouge paw.[†12]

Ms. Hamilton was among the first makeup artists, which added a new position to the growing army of beauty experts.

Instruction on beauty culture for the laywoman also took the form of the self-help seminar and multilevel marketing scheme, offering in-person lectures that promised to reveal the secrets of skin care, comportment, style, and proper application of products. Mme. Yale, "The Queen of Beauty," for example, offered the women of Boston, Massachusetts, insight into "God's Purpose for Beauty"[13] and attendees in Omaha, Nebraska, "Object Lessons in Beauty Culture."[14] Tickets were free, but guests probably had some difficulty escaping without laying down a dollar or two on "Madame Yale's Jack Rose Bud Lip Tint" or "Bust Food," which was also available on special that week at nearby Houghton & Dutton's Department Store.[15] Movies wouldn't have sound for almost three decades, TV wasn't even a future fantasy, and yet somehow Madame Yale already had pioneered a sort of infomercial. If the consumer boom years of those first decades of the twentieth century put wheels on the newborn American advertising industry, the cosmetics business was already giving it wings.

Makeup artists, hairdressers, and aestheticians were increasingly not only given the role of experts in the popular narrative, but they were imbued with magical, fairy godmother–like abilities to transform women. At the same time, the media began to traffic in the trope that feminists were the adversaries of beauty, all grim seriousness and "broad flat shoes."[16] Bring the concepts together, and you have one of the first references to the sort of makeovers that would fuel magazines and movie plots for decades to come. In an anonymously sourced article for the *Chicago Daily Tribune*, one beauty specialist lamented that she had her work cut out for her with

---

† They literally mean paw. In addition to being a good-luck token, rabbit's feet were often used to apply blush before being replaced by other, better natural-hair or synthetic brushes.

suffragist visits. "I have a suffrage visit this morning . . . and though I shudder a little at the prospect, yet I smile at the same time for I know I shall succeed at my task." Adding that after years of self-imposed frumpiness, the client had come to realize that to really prosper at anything in this world, one had to be conventionally presentable. "They have a feeling that dowdiness and woman suffrage go together. It is necessary if we wish to be successful that we overcome that notion."[17] Stories like these were inextricably linking a certain type of feminine beauty with power, respectability, and upward mobility, and that message was, for better or worse, being received by everyone to some degree.

Black women in particular were awash in cosmetics both as a form of uplift for the opportunities they provided and a de facto kind of oppression due to the white supremacist standard of American beauty. It was a frustration they began to voice in the early years of the twentieth century. Regarding several letters to the editor on the subject of beautifiers used to catch and keep a husband, the editor of the Black-owned paper, the *Star of Zion*, responded:

> It is in our interest then to make ourselves beautiful. If nature failed in supplying us, let us resort to art. Negro men as a rule, claim that women of the Caucasian race make kinder, better, more affectionate wives. We beg to differ. Fortunately, the women referred to use more cosmetics, false hair and hair growers in six months than we do in twelve, because we can't afford to buy 'em and most husbands won't buy 'em for us. The white women by the use of these articles soften their features, supply all deficiencies, add to their looks, and their beauty deceives man, deludes him, and makes him believe they are angels walking about on this earth. No use talking, a well-groomed, sweet-voiced woman has her way; and the [paper's] advice to all women is, make attractive yourselves, all that bosh . . . to the contrary notwithstanding. Inherit beauty if you can; but by all means get it.[18]

Lipstick and powder barely hit the shelves as mass market items, and they were already problematic. Disappointing but hardly surprising in an economy that bombarded consumers every day with racist images that advertised everything from cereal to tobacco. Even cosmetic companies that specifically catered to women of color, like Kashmir, would continue to offer items such as "whitener" that held up the Jim Crow ideal of beauty.

Successful African American beauty entrepreneurs, like Madam C. J. Walker,‡ would continue to feel the push and pull of providing their consumers with what they were told they wanted and declaring their worth on their own terms for most of the next century. Despite the seemingly insurmountable obstacles, Black women would continue to forge paths through the beauty industry as practitioners and purchasers in a way that would make their mark indelible.

So with all of this media coverage and makeup artists and special jewelry, wearing lipstick was now widely accepted and everyone was doing it, right? Short answer: no. Long answer: it was moving forward but still weighed down by much of the same baggage as the generation before. Yes for the socialite; maybe for the working woman; no for the housewife. Also, no for the suffragist and yes for the actress. There's no one narrative yet, rather, each segment of media developed according to its audience and vice versa. The arguments against were still largely a continuation of Victorian debates as to whether it was a deceptive practice or whether it should be a well-hidden secret. The arguments for included the notion that lipstick was modern, flattering, and a must-have for the busy woman. The former also included a camp of critics that fell into a category that could be described as "paint if you must, but do so flawlessly," adding this to the list of womanly skills like fashion, cooking, homemaking, and child-rearing at which women were expected to naturally excel by virtue of birth and reading the right magazines.

In Baltimore, Maryland, the *Sun* equivocated, "'Shall I makeup or not?' It is a burning question for many women, and one they must answer themselves,"[19] while the *Daily Home News* of New Brunswick, New Jersey harumphed,[20] "For the average woman who uses cosmetics does not know how to put them on. She deceives no one but herself, and at the best is only a good advertisement of artificial beauty. At no time does she resemble the real thing." The *Pittsburgh Press* continued to moralize and explained that in the words of Reverend Christian F. Reisner, makeup

---

‡ Madam Walker largely made her fortune in hair care, not color cosmetics, but her success was so enormous and precedent setting that it's really worth celebrating as a model for the industry. Born to former slaves as Sarah Breedlove in 1867, her business empire would come to encompass both products and beauty schools employing thousands and making her one of America's first self-made female millionaires and philanthropists during an era in which she couldn't legally walk through the front door of most establishments.

was artifice and "No lasting love can be built upon a lie, however trivial."[21] On the other hand, within a couple years the very same paper would insist, "You must remember that using rouge is not a matter of morality but a question of taste."[22] Pshaw to all of that, said fashion-forward *Vogue*, declaring in an article that "the Old Order passes" and "No longer in the secret fastness of the *boudoir* but boldly before the curious eye of the public is the bloom of beauty applied to cheek and lip."[23]

Lipstick—particularly *reapplying* lipstick—was increasingly normalized as a part of everyday grooming, and a good chunk of that can be attributed to another pair of technical advances, the tube and the motion picture. The former has many fathers and even more patents, and the lat-

W. G. KENDALL.
LIP STICK HOLDER.
APPLICATION FILED JAN. 25, 1917.

1,236,846.

Patented Aug. 14, 1917.

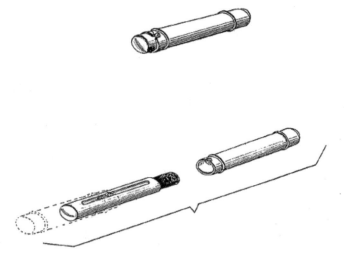

Now we're going places. Mechanical illustration for the first push-up lipstick. This innovative case would make lipstick more portable, taking it out of the boudoir and into public. *U.S. Patent Office*

ter is credited to Thomas Edison.§ The lipstick tube is a little hazier. By 1911 retailers like Sears Roebuck & Company were offering a "Fine Lip Rouge" in a long, round metal container, but there's no specific patent on file, so no credit can be given.

Similar forms would be on the market for years when in 1917 the U.S. Patent Office issued patent number 1,236,846 to one Mr. W. G. Kendall of Newark, New Jersey for his "Lip Stick Holder," which consisted of a cap, a case, and a platform that raised and lowered the product by means of a tiny tab pushed up or down in a channel on the side of the case. In other words, a primitive version of the lipstick with which we're pretty much all familiar. "My present invention relates to new and useful improvements in holders for lip sticks of rouge," he humbly presented in his patent application, "the primary object of my invention being the provision of a neat, ornamental and serviceable lip stick holder which may be cheaply manufactured and readily assembled." Mission accomplished! It didn't make him a household name or a millionaire and it didn't even seem to remain his exclusive intellectual property for very long, but it did exactly what it was designed to do, making lipstick a portable, affordable item that could be tucked easily and neatly into purses, dressers, glove boxes, and desks across America.

Mr. Edison's motion pictures, in addition to their myriad other charms, gave women both a place to wear lipstick and a reason to do so. In less than one generation, America had filled with movie theaters and, more importantly, movie fans with an insatiable appetite for any information about their favorite stars. This was such a new phenomenon, in fact, that the studios themselves had to learn how to handle it. At first, actors often weren't even named in the credits of their pictures, leading to one of the first stars with a large fan base to become known as the "Biograph Girl," after the studio she worked for. Not just odd considering her drawing power but also kind of a waste, given that her legal name, Florence Lawrence, sounded like a stage name. Movie impresarios quickly realized their error and soon began cultivating their stars' recognizability with no small measure of help from the newly minted movie magazines that were now flooding newsstands.

---

§ Edison was as much master publicist as inventor, so even though the first viable motion picture camera emerged from his labs and into the patent office in 1893, it was actually one of his employees, Edward Kennedy Laurie Dickson, who developed it.

Fantasy was now an industry. In addition to providing reviews and industry news, fan magazines filled their pulpy pages with articles that covered both the lavish details of stars' gowns, homes, and social lives and the do-it-yourself style pieces that let readers live the fantasy and the glamour on a shoestring. Makeup really lent itself to this format. If a reader couldn't have the latest eveningwear from Paris, she could still head down to the five-and-dime and treat herself to a new lipstick and learn how to apply it like her favorite actress. In 1916, as communist Emma Goldman was being arrested for publicly lecturing on birth control and World War I raged across Europe, *Photoplay* was offering subscribers the movie-approved way to apply lipstick: "As to the mouth. Here the makeup is too often apparent and badly done. Those who wish an obviously artificial appearance accent this particular feature, but for those who do not, this advice is given: do not depend on the lip stick."[24] *Picture-Play* magazine encouraged women to think of themselves as potential starlets through the power of color as explained by actress Alice Joyce: "To a girl who contemplates a career in the silent drama; makeup and makeup methods will prove one of the greatest surprises and most interesting phases of her work. . . . In these days of rouge and lip stick when approximately 60% of femininity, apply color to their cheeks, eyebrows, and lips, you would think make-up was a widely understood thing, it is not."[25] The upshot is that if you did understand how to apply makeup, you too could have fame and fortune. No matter how unlikely, the democratic fairy tale that just about anyone could be a star with the right makeup and a big break would fuel the synergy between beauty and motion pictures for decades to come.

In 1917, *Picture-Play* magazine noted that "Theda Bara has transferred her lip rouge, her bizarre gowns, and her own bewitching personality to the sun-kissed hills of California."[26] She, like so many others attached to the business, made the move west not for the change of climate but because the motion picture industry itself was becoming "Hollywood" and the studios were relocating their productions facilities. Bara herself, born Theodosia Goodman¶ in 1885, was one of the industry's earliest and greatest successes in creating sex symbols. By far the most enduring screen "vamp," or vampire woman, she was often (but not always) cast as a heartless siren who

---

¶ The name Theda Bara has alternately been suggested to have come from her childhood nickname plus a version of her grandfather's last name (Barranger) or an anagram for "Arab death."

The vamp. Movie star Theda Bara's onscreen "vampire woman" persona (seen here in 1917's *Cleopatra*) would define the era and influence generations of beauty fans. *Wikimedia Commons*

seduced, destroyed, and tossed men away without a second thought. It was a role her studio bosses insisted she play off-screen, too, and the look that went along with the persona would become iconic, eventually inspiring homage from pop culture figures from Marilyn Monroe to Siouxsie Sioux. To maintain the illusion of exotic origins, public relations let it be known she was the daughter of a sheik and a French woman and was raised in the Sahara, which was far sexier than the plain truth, which was that she was the daughter of a prosperous Jewish tailor from Cincinnati, Ohio. Her innovative version of the darkly shaded eye, pale skin, and blood-red lip would be de rigueur for youth cultures from flappers to goths for the next century, whether they were aware of it or not.

Vamp wasn't the only look Hollywood was selling. There was also the fresh-scrubbed, girl-next-door appeal of actresses like America's sweetheart, Mary Pickford (who is largely remembered for playing little girls into her late twenties) and scores of other starlets. Whatever flavor it took, motion pictures were selling beauty and selling it hard. From early on the movie business realized it was box office gold for everyone to be in cahoots with the beauty industry. Some forms were gentle, like distributors suggesting that for showings of *Cleopatra*,** theater owners cross-sell with drugstores, "Get the store handling cosmetics to hook with you in window displays and loan them photographs."[27] While some ventures were more (literally) in your face, with the stars endorsing products that also happened to mention their studio or upcoming attraction. Such arrangements were few at this time but were about to explode within the next few years thanks in no small part to the savvy of a Polish-born makeup artist, Maksimillian Faktorowicz.

The escapism of movies had arrived just in time for many fans, since outside of the dream factory, America would soon face some hard times. After years of isolationist arguments, America finally entered World War I officially on April 6, 1917. As if that didn't visit enough death and destruction on all involved, the globe found itself suffering under the scourge of a worldwide pandemic barely a year later. In earlier times, either of these events could have derailed lipstick as a fashion or grooming item, but its roots were now strong enough to weather the onslaught of wartime scarcity and the hygienic concerns of a flood of deadly influenza casualties.

Although not used or credited as extensively as during World War II, the war effort for World War I would, of course, rely on the labor and support of women in traditionally male roles at home. In addition, lipstick would help in its own informal way by virtue of Congress's 5 percent tax hike on all cosmetics (as well as other manufactured goods)[28] to support the expenses of freeing Europe from the Hun, which was estimated to add an impressive $4.75 million[29] to the nation's coffers. Motion pictures, jewelry, and chewing gum were somehow exempt from bankrolling the great war.[30] In terms of their actual work, one critic wryly noted that women might be naturally suited to camouflage due to their experience with makeup and clothing. "In the face of facts, is there any denying that the fairer sex are adept in the old art with a new name. . . . Lip stick and powder puff have been discarded for the paint brush. The boudoir negligee is replaced by heavy overalls or military uniform and girls today are responsible for some of the best military camouflage work that is being done in America." The author may have been being cute, but she also meant

---

** The picture referenced here is not Theda Bara's version of *Cleopatra* made the same year, but one that was made in 1912 starring another screen vamp, Helen Gardner, and rereleased to cash in on the success of Bara's version. Gardner's 1912 version was restored in 2000; sadly, just a few fragments of Bara's iteration survive.

it literally, noting that "The first camouflage corps for women began its training in New York on April 1, since that date numerous organizations have come into being in other sections of the country."[31]

In addition to skilled workers, women served as clerks and support staff at home. In theater, nurses in particular were crucial to keeping the war machine humming. In a nod to morale, the uniform, and the fact that they were in the middle of a literal war zone, most beautifiers were left at home. However, "All manage, no matter the nature of their work, to be neat and clean as circumstances permit, and they are 'wisely careful of the appearance of nails and knuckles and have not discarded all that was good in manicuring.' But the only cosmetics they use are rainwater and face creams for chapping and sunburn."[32] Not a standard our men in uniform were held to, but a sign that only so much femininity could be dropped at any given moment, even in service to the greater good.

Women on the home front had mixed feelings about giving up lipstick and other small luxuries, and there was some encouragement to do so, although no formal rationing of food and consumer items. Instead, to ensure they had the materials they needed and the financial support of the populace, the government relied on a combination of propaganda and goodwill. Ladies, like those of the Wichita Society, felt that they could meet the moment and support the nation by scrimping on beauty and fashion. One member proudly declaring, "In this time, when a great hour of history is at hand, there is a united sentiment of women in this city to do away with glitter and tinsel, to put aside trivial things. The women of Wichita will practice economy in the kitchen and in dress. Like the French women, the women of Wichita will learn to carry the weight of war instead of the lip-stick."[33] Without specific scrap metal programs or fundraising initiatives, how giving up lipstick was helpful to the cause is not entirely clear, but the symbolism was still powerful. Lipstick was now synonymous with womanhood and all the accoutrements that came along with that construct; offering to give it up was clearly a gesture displaying no small measure of patriotic weight.

It was also the sort of move that must have scared manufacturers to death, since they had staked their fortunes on the lipstick trend. Luckily for them, Uncle Sam took a laissez-faire attitude toward consumer spending in those days and was hesitant to even designate what a luxury looked like during the course of the war. According to W. S. Gifford, the director of the Council of National Defense, "We cannot say certain things are a luxury and none must buy them on that account. What is a luxury to one person is almost a necessity to another. There is ample room for widespread economy and thrift without destroying particular industries."[34] All of which boiled down to makeup companies continuing to be able to churn out their goods and consumers being able to snap them up—all in their own frugal way, of course.

The war didn't stop the beauty trade, and surprisingly it's very hard to say what impact, if any, the 1918 pandemic had on lipstick sales. Mask wearing, quarantine, and the low morale of the nation in general certainly decreased interest and sales for a time, but there's very little specific reference to wearing lipstick itself as a problem. Female vanity is often one of the first things scrutinized during times of crisis, with critics asking if women are too loose, too narcissistic, or too ambitious for the greater good, but for whatever reason, lipstick (and most fashion for that matter) escaped attack. There continued to be the usual criticisms of makeup wearing as fundamentally dishonest, poorly done, or morally questionable, but there was little (if any) mass media concern about lipstick and hygiene or physical decay. Lipstick (now also known as lip-stick and lip stick) would survive to see another day.

America would not just come back from those dark years, she would thrive. The days after the armistice on November 11, 1918, would find the spirit of the nation both broken and reborn, launching it into a period that would be defined by the struggle between our strict puritan roots and our craving for everything modern and novel. For a large percentage of the female population, the newfound right to make their mark on the world would be enshrined in law, soaked in gin, and written in bright red letters.

CHAPTER FOUR

THE GLOSSED GENERATION
The 1920s

Shades of the Decade
Pert Rouge Rose
Princess Pat Vivid
Helena Rubinstein Red Geranium
Bourjois Ashes of Roses
Coty Dark Cerise

A t the beginning of the 1921 school year, Miss Pearl Pugsley of Knobel, Arkansas, was sent home from high school for wearing lipstick and powder. Not only were her parents understanding about her common, minor adolescent infraction, they retained a lawyer on her behalf. Their daughter's civil rights had been grossly violated and, if need be, they would fight the school district all the way to the Supreme Court to restore them.[1] Thus began yet another skirmish in the little known but not historically insignificant "lipstick wars" of the Jazz Age. Sadly, there are no bronze statues of Pearl and her sisters in arms, no solemn national holidays remembering her stand, but at the time there was no shortage of nationwide press coverage of her position on personal freedoms and the ensuing court proceedings. Which was perhaps to be expected given the zeitgeist; America itself had reached a sort of collective adolescence with some very modern rights and very old-fashioned restrictions. The 1920s opened with two deeply consequential Constitutional

43

amendments: the Nineteenth Amendment, which assured women (white women mainly, although not specifically) the right to vote and the Eighteenth Amendment, which enshrined the prohibition of liquor sales as a matter of law. The resulting period tested the boundaries of both American's newfound freedom and long-held traditions. Given the context—a country that had survived both the serious business of a world war and a devastating pandemic, it's a small wonder that Pearl's inflated act of rebellion gained momentum. America seemed to be very much in the mood for some well-earned silliness.

At the height of her fame, according to her mother, Pearl was offered "$1,000 a week" by a "Los Angeles motion picture concern [that] wants 'the heroine of the lipstick war.'"[2] Although no motion picture seems to have resulted from her legal dramas, the budding flapper did achieve short-lived notoriety, with a "half ton" of letters wishing her well. She had, after all, added to the public conversation surrounding cosmetics, telling a San Diego paper that it was more than vanity—that there was a principle at stake. "It wasn't a desire to create trouble when the suit was filed,' she explained. 'I merely felt my toes were being trampled on, so to speak, and the Irish blood in me began to boil. I'm going to fight the case to a finish in an effort to uphold women's rights to use all reasonable means to look their best at all times.'"[3] Ultimately, her siege ended in 1923 with a whimper and not a bang, when the Arkansas Supreme Court decided that "Courts have other and more important functions to perform than that of hearing the complaints of disaffected pupils of the public schools against rules and regulations promulgated by the school boards for the government of the schools."[4] Her request denied, Pearl faded into obscurity, yet another fallen foot soldier in one of the many "lipstick wars" of the day.

Given her tender age and the recent passage of women's suffrage, it really wasn't that farfetched for Pearl to associate women's rights to beauty with women's rights to full citizenship. There had been, in fact, some overlap of the two in the papers. One editorial page, in Pearl's own home state of Arkansas, held that now was a good time to warn the rest of the electorate that feminine wiles could be an undue influence on political discourse. "With the national enfranchisement of women, the old discussion arises as to whether women will rely upon the frills, the lipstick, the sidelong glance, and the silk stocking to get votes for themselves or their favorite candidates."[5] With no experience of women as a voting bloc or as elected officials, the prospect of a lady vote could mean anything. For some writers, it clearly had something to do with cosmetics, because that was already shorthand for the female experience.

> With universal suffrage, it is recognized that there may soon be a feminine scramble for office. And there is fear expressed in some quarters that women will have men at a disadvantage. A writer in the *New York Times* suggests that "the female body politic will avail itself of all the weapons at its command in future political contests. Rouge and the lipstick will play their full part. A peaches-and-cream complexion will be a great asset to a politician."[6]

These fears turned out to be unfounded. A century after that writing, despite some great strides, there's still no female candidate whose makeup has been deemed good enough to capture the presidency.

For those celebrating the passage of the Eighteenth Amendment, makeup also was much on their minds, albeit not in a celebratory way. Having achieved its goal of banishing liquor from America, the Women's Christian Temperance Union (WCTU) was in search of new quests and there was talk of going to war against the scourge of makeup. In 1921, when the ink (and the country) was barely dry on the Prohibition Act, WCTU officer Mrs. George F. Pashley made a primordial argument against what modern gender critics would call "the male gaze,"* stating that women should relinquish their need to be attractive to men in order to advance in work and politics. In her estimation, "Whatever has been done to lift womankind from the plane of a parasitic creature has been done by woman herself. She will get no encouragement from mankind in a war on the lipstick. If it is to be abolished, woman will do it herself."[7] Ahead of its time as a feminist critique, it also brutally removed agency from women in their choice to wear makeup or not. Her quest was labeled a full-on "Lipstick War" by the papers.[8] In a gentler rebuke, another officer, "Dr. P.S. Bourdeau-Sisco feminine," declared at the organization's 1921 national meeting in San Francisco, "Let's go after the lipstick, and the rouge, and these other beautifying instruments. There is no room for

---

* Popularized by film critic Laura Mulvey, the "male gaze" theory holds that most visual arts and literature caters to the viewpoint of straight men by presenting women as passive sex objects for their consumption.

smeared lips in America."[9] In the end, the national organization declined to include lipstick on the same list as "demon rum," though not due to any sense of solidarity with flappers. One of the higher-ups simply decided, "The women who use lip-stick are not the sort we can educate. Their feet are firmly set on the road of folly they have selected for themselves. Their brains are not big enough to grasp the truth about themselves. So, we must let them go. They are hopeless."[10] History correctly remembers that the prohibitionists were not a lot of fun.

On the flip side of nearly everything the WCTU stood for were flappers—not an organized movement as such, but rather a style or an attitude that would define young women for almost a decade. Although the flapper's pursuits were perhaps less focused and not as profound as the suffrage and civil rights movements of earlier decades, there is a great deal to be said for the personal freedoms for women that the flappers embodied. For a certain segment of the population during the twenties, it became all the rage to attend college, date widely, speak freely, and generally follow one's own muse, even if that just meant smoking cigarettes in public, listening to jazz, and drinking bootleg liquor. There was also a certain democracy in being a flapper, since it could be adapted to some extent to suit every woman from the debutante to the shopgirl; there were flappers of color in the Harlem Renaissance and farm girl flappers who dreamed of becoming Hollywood starlets. The demure appeal of the corseted Gibson girl was a thing of the past; the young women with rolled stockings, bobbed hair, and wild energy of "flaming youth"† were now calling the shots.

Fashion and fad may have defined them, but it also freed them. They were the first generation of American women to widely reject the confines of the corset and petticoat in favor of looser, more comfortable dresses and flexible undergarments; to cut their hair into shorter "boyish" bobs; and to adopt the painted, bee-stung lip as their calling card. In other words, they were going to hell *or* the kids were alright, depending on which cultural critic you were listening to. "The lipstick queen sitting in the place formerly occupied by modest maidens. Sunday papers carried under arms that formerly carried Bibles"[11] charged Reverend Robert McCaul in a sermon denouncing New York City as the new Babylon. On the contrary,

---

† The term itself comes from Samuel Hopkins Adams's era-defining 1923 novel (and the subsequent film of the same name) that preached a sort of sexual liberation without moralistic consequence, which was a revolutionary concept for American audiences at the time.

said Reverend Claude E. Morris, emphasizing temperance when it came to the fashions of the day, "Most girls do use lip-stick, rouge, and eyebrow pencil. In moderation. I believe these harmless cosmetics improve their looks. Personally, I approve the moderate use of them by girls and young married women." In his opinion, you didn't run into trouble with makeup until you were wearing enough to emulate "chorus girls."[12]

"Should the flapper with her elaborate makeup, her elaborate clothes, her bold and confident carriage, be suppressed as a menace to the nation's morals, or celebrated as its chief claim to art and beauty?" asked syndicated columnist, Frederic J. Haskin.[13] Ultimately, he concluded that flappers were an asset to the country, since they added youthful exuberance and if not natural beauty, certainly more of it. The old guard was learning to live with its noisy new residents and their antics. As for the new guard, they were bolstered by seeing themselves reflected in the fashion pages, in store windows, over the airwaves, and on the silver screen.

Flappers, no matter what you thought of their morals, bought stuff from Coca-Cola to cold cream, and manufacturers were not about to let the golden opportunity to woo new customers pass them by. In 1920 it was estimated that American women (and probably a few men) spent a collective "$750,000,000 for rouge, lipsticks, powder, and perfume during 1919 according to a compilation of luxury tax returns at the Treasury today."[14] Which was no small chunk of change for a population that was about 105,711,000[15] persons and growing rapidly. These expenditures were not just good for the economy, as one editorial entitled "How Poor We Are!" suggested, they were a much-needed bulwark against Bolshevik influence. "Yes, the socialist orators tell us that the people of America are being ground under the heel of capitalism and their lot is a deplorable one. They make it a lot more emphatic than that. And yet American women paid $750,000,000 for rouge, lipsticks, powder, and perfume during 1919."[16] Lipstick was now as political as it was popular, and this was hardly the last time it would be cast as a cosmetic with the power to defeat communism (and later fascism and then communism again).

American consumers were now purchasing makeup at such an impressive clip that some critics were concerned about how much they were literally consuming. "Eats Her Height in Lipstick Every Four Years" blared one headline. "Iowa dealers in cosmetics declare that the modern girl requires six lipsticks a year to maintain the kissable, cupid's bow mouth which so tantalizes her admirers with its flaming hue. Their tabulations indicate that miss four feet tall actually eats her own height in lipstick every four years."[17] All of which was sensational, if true. However, the measurements used seem a bit unusual: the average American woman was already more than five feet tall, and even before the invention of long-wear lipstick, replacing your color twelve times a day as the article suggests seems highly impractical.

Even so, lipstick ingredients were largely benign, despite a couple glaring exceptions. Another estimation posited that "The amount of lipstick men have 'eaten' inadvertently while kissing these ladies and the amount that these ladies have 'eaten' inadvertently by moistening with their tongues would probably total several tons a year."[18] All of which was based on the supposedly reassuring fact that "Fifty Million Painted Lips Kissed Everyday!—And No One Gets Poisoned." Strangely put and largely true, the thought was probably reassuring to a measure of the population, which for generations had been told that makeup contained lead, arsenic, and other toxins.

In addition to the spending spree on cosmetics, the 1920s also marked the years during which America tipped from a majority rural population to a primarily urban one,[19] putting more people closer to a range of goods, services, and social activities from which they'd previously been cut off. Taken together, the post–World War I outlook was an advertiser's dream: a growing economy and a free-spending populace with leisure time and an eye for novelty. This worked out especially well for one city in particular: Hollywood. Both the city of Los Angeles itself, which was expanding along with other metropolitan areas, but more importantly, the concept of Hollywood: the movies and their reach in terms of cultural influence.

As a tastemaker, Hollywood was beginning to develop savvy for its potential markets. So much so that it was reaching beyond its roster of star performers to make a celebrity out of a behind-the-scenes player. Not just a smart move in terms of providing the industry with new revenue and marketing channels, it also fit nicely into the entrepreneur mythos that has long driven American business, the force that made Thomas Edison and Henry Ford household names. It's no exaggeration to say that the fully Americanized Max Factor—who was born in 1877 as Maksimilian Faktorowicz in Poland—would revolutionize the formulas, techniques, and sale of makeup for generations to come. By the time he came to national attention, there were no doubt hundreds of makeup artists working in Hollywood, but he was one of the few to become and remain a household name. A lot of this can be traced to some very smart legend building via media and advertising.

Before 1925, Max Factor's name mainly appears in industry directories, where he advertised his eponymous "House of Makeup" next to classifieds for a "Big Tame Bear" and "Oriental Costumes" for rent.[20] From that Los Angeles shop he supplied makeup and wigs for a number of movie studios and was a favorite in the trade for his skill. His big break came in 1923 as part of a technological breakthrough in movie making, specifically panchromatic film, which did a better job of capturing actors' faces. However, it presented a real problem initially. Previously, film actors had been encased in such thick layers of grease paint and powder that early lighting tests with the higher-resolution film made them look positively ghoulish. In response, Factor emerged from his laboratory with a thinner, more flexible foundation that would ultimately take the commercial name Pancake Makeup.[21] This breakthrough solidified his place in the industry as a genius. From there, he built a reputation as *the* Hollywood glamour expert and released a line of mass-market cosmetics that were initially sold as "Max Factor Supreme Toiletries"[22] until his name alone was enough to propel them.

The recipe for success came together at the right time and managed to combine several factors that had already worked for the industry into one mega-watt advertising scheme: celebrity endorsement, trusted expertise, the entrepreneur story, and a do-it-yourself moxie with an all-American twist. In one article, which identified him as "famous cosmetician of the West," Factor claimed "America is becoming the cosmetic producing center of the world. Paris is fighting desperately to overcome the commanding position the United States is taking in this art, on which Parisians once had a monopoly."[23] In an era during which America really was feeling her power, this was a true selling point—any American miss on Main Street could now consider herself on par with the sophistication and fashion savvy of any mademoiselle strolling the boulevards of Paris.

That said, he did see one area where Americans had fallen down on the job. "One of the worst calamities to have befallen the beauty of American womanhood is the lack of education about the application of makeup."[24] Luckily, his company could fix that. A number of Max Factor–approved emissaries were trained and dispatched across the country, where local ads featured a star of a recent studio release and, more intriguingly, upcoming in-store events in which these artists revealed the secrets of "how he made her so beautiful" and how "he makes up many of the movie stars—conceals their bad points, accentuates their good ones—with wonderful Max Factor makeup."[25] He was selling the fantasy in a way that female movie lovers could easily grasp: all that Hollywood glamour could be yours whether you lived in Washington, D.C., or Des Moines, for just the cost of a 50-cent lipstick.[26] Plus, since it was taught by an expert, it could be reasoned this was not simply an exercise in vanity, it was a virtuous investment in self-improvement, another American favorite.

Over the years, the company would continue to be top industry player and to perfect its messaging around the elements of Tinseltown credibility, celebrity endorsement, and achievable simplicity. His early fan magazine ads were a cavalcade of stars, including a young Joan Crawford, who was still in her flapper "cupid's bow" lipstick phase—her signature exaggerated lip line would come later—and an advertorial with actress (and the mistress of media magnate William Randolph Hearst) Marion Davies.

Marion Davies wants some girl among motion picture audiences to win her complete $50.00 Max Factor Makeup Kit. The kit will be awarded to the best letter, not exceeding 300 words in length, answering Miss Davies' question: Does the correct use of makeup double a pretty girl's beauty and make any woman, no matter how unattractive, really lovely?

Three hundred words gave contestants a significant amount of space to answer "yes." The takeaway really was that makeup, well applied, was its own sort of magic.

In order to ensure that every customer could achieve that wizardry for herself, Max Factor created a foolproof system. He divided every woman into one of four categories of "Color Harmony," and consumers simply picked their shades along the lines of blonde, brunette, brownette (a.k.a. auburn), and red. The ads in fan magazines promised the stars' own secrets and took full advantage of their favorite actresses' signature strengths. "Hollywood's makeup king offers you a new secret of beauty . . . powder, lipstick and rouge and other essentials, created in varied color harmonies to blend perfectly with every variation of complexion coloring."[27] Sort of. It worked for a lot of women; however, in retrospect, it may have been a little too simple, since it left out any crossover and a huge percentage of women of color. Undeterred, women of color forged ahead in the quest for glamour either by purchasing from companies that didn't acknowledge them as an audience or by patronizing a number of smaller companies with lower price points that did and turned to newspapers and magazines that spoke to their concerns. Outside of those specialized venues, it would be a long time before the mainstream press and mass market or luxury brands would factor in a wider range of skin tones and tastes for Black, Asian, Latinx, and other consumers.

Outside of the movies, the 1920s were a boom time for other forms of celebrity culture. One particularly popular favorite was the daredevil: flyers, adventurers, pole sitters, and rumrunners all had their moment in the spotlight. Combine that with flapper sex appeal and add a little

The high-flying flapper. Ruth Elder would not be the first female solo pilot to cross the Atlantic, but her unflagging dedication to lipstick would bring an element of glamour to international travel and embody the freedom of the era. *The Ruth Elder Project*

Hollywood glamour, and you had a real sensation. Enter Ruth Elder. Although less remembered than her contemporary, Amelia Earhart, Elder was an early aviation pioneer and lipstick superfan. She had been working as an assistant in a Florida dentist's office when Charles Lindbergh completed his first transatlantic flight. Swept up in the excitement (and possibly looking for a way to break into the movies), she and her husband began flying lessons. In the summer of 1927, after two years of training, she declared that she was ready to take on the challenge. She may have been under some pressure to get going, since a Russian émigré named Liuba Phillips was challenging her quest to become the first woman to navigate the Atlantic, and there was little notoriety in being the second to do something, no matter how dangerous.[28] After acquiring a plane, which she dubbed *American Girl*, she announced she would "hop off" for Paris from New York in mid-September. Delayed by inclement weather, she was grounded in New York for several weeks, which gave her enough time to become something of a fixation with the national press, which reported on her divorce, her beauty pageant win, and her previous career choices. Delayed again on October 1, the press instead reported on her preparations, noting that "Besides her flying suit, Miss Elder will take, she said, two dresses, a powder puff, a lip stick, and a mirror."[29]

Finally, on October 12, New York's *Daily News* announced in all caps: "Flapper Wings for Paris."[30] She almost made it. Sometime in the early morning hours of October 13, Ruth and her copilot, George Haldeman, struggling with ice on the wings and a broken oil line, crash-landed the *American Girl* in the Atlantic Ocean off the Azores, where a Dutch steamer picked them up unharmed.[31]

> "Thank you very much" were her first words when she and Haldeman were taken aboard the Dutch tanker *Bahrendrecht* on Thursday, the crew said today. Then she produced her lipstick apparently oblivious to the fact that she had stepped from the very jaws of death to safety. So deep an impression did her *sangfroid* in the face of the great danger she had just escaped, make on the crew that the lipstick episode was duly noted in an official summary of the rescue as given out to the *Bahrendrecht*'s radio operator.[32]

Ruth was, so to speak, unflappable.

Ruth Elder wouldn't become the first "woman flyer" to solo navigate the Atlantic—that distinction would go to Amelia Earhart the next year—but she made a big enough splash to earn herself a small-time movie career, a glittering trip to Paris, and a huge amount of media attention. Although not well-known today, Ruth was truly emblematic of her era in which women were trying to balance new-found freedom against long-held expectations of femininity. It's a dichotomy both enthralling and exhausting for those trying to manage it either in the spotlight or in their own personal way: go for it, but make sure you look cute while doing so. It's a balance that women are still trying to strike, and for the women of the next decade, who faced some of the darkest days in American history for female ambition and financial security, it would be even tougher. America's women, like Ruth's *American Girl*, were about to hit some rough seas. Although youth culture always exists in some form, the Depression would effectively kill off the flapper in the wild and set back some of the progress women had made in the public sphere due both to economic necessity and social backlash. At the end of the decade that gave them the vote and celebrated their buying power, women could now safely consider lipstick the norm. Soon, the focus of mass media conversation about lipstick would shift away from whether one should use makeup and toward how to keep up, because women were going places and lipstick was coming along.

CHAPTER FIVE
IN THE RED
The 1930s

Shades of the Decade
Tangee Theatrical Red
Max Factor Brownette
Tattoo Exotic
Elizabeth Arden Coronation Red
Helena Rubenstein Red Coral

If an era can be said to have ended in an afternoon, the Jazz Age played its last with the clanging of the closing bell of the stock market on October 29, 1929. The implosion of the capital markets that had fueled the go-go-go ethos of the 1920s meant that America was now depressed—both financially and in spirit. "Flaming youth" was over, replaced by the "forgotten man" and his forsaken female counterpart. After working so hard to establish itself as an industry and an entity, would lipstick take a hit as another victim of hard times? The answer was simply *no*. As part of the package of modernity, cosmetic beauty would not only survive, but flourish. Always at the cutting edge, the fashion bible *Vogue* recognized the moment women found themselves in—by 1931, it declared in its "Beauty Gospels" that "Of all make-up nothing is as significant as our lipsticks. If we were perpetuating gestures of the twentieth century for posterity certainly putting on lipstick would head the list."[1]

Tough times would prove a boon for cosmetics, in part because the industry had spent the years between the suffragists and the flappers making their products an indispensable, inevitable part of the female experience—*not* wearing lipstick was now the statement (and not one a respectable woman wanted to make) plus now was no time for going au naturel, when a woman's own personal boom or bust could depend on a well-painted face. Less than two decades into its acceptance as an every-day essential like toothpaste or electricity, lipstick was already assuming the weight of obligation and expectation of products specifically marketed to women. Lipstick's advent came with the now constant mass media chatter that promised both to emancipate one's true power as a woman and to make her acceptable to the patriarchy. So which was it? Like most changes that redefined the contours of what it meant to be female in the world, it was a little bit of both. For a new generation of women, lipstick now represented some very modern aspirations: economic independence, self-expression, and a knowing sex appeal. On the other hand, it also meant a nonstop mission to fit a very narrow definition of beauty that was marked by worship of an ideal that was white, effortlessly flawless, upwardly mobile, young, and straight. Either model of womanhood was a hard target to hit, but as in the movies of the era, women were taught in ways great and small to paint on a smile, keep their chin up, and keep on trying—and maybe tap dance.

Hard times called for glamour more than ever. For thousands of women whose reality resembled a Dorothea Lange dustbowl portrait, their fantasy was the unflappable, unruffled, unstoppable career gals Hollywood churned out by the score. Depression be damned, the gleaming, streamlined push for modernity, femininity, and "it" continued apace, entering a new era wherein lipstick would move beyond social statement and into absolute necessity with record numbers of women entering the workforce. Barely a year into the economic downturn, the *New York Times* declared that "Women of America Are Not Cutting Down on Cosmetics, Manufacturers Are Told." According to industry expert B. F. Breslauer, the average American woman spent about $150 a year (at a time when the approximate average household income was around $1,300), which "has not been decreased, first because in itself is not a tremendous sum for them, second because they cannot afford to look less attractive at the present time with the need of getting jobs and the competition in holding husbands or sweethearts."[2] While the author demurred on the expense of a complexion soap here and new shade of lipstick there, it was actually a huge outlay for those actually facing financial hardship of unemployment or under-employment. The money spent, however, could be viewed as the cost of doing business as a female—it was simply the barrier to entry into the working world. Beauty, it would seem, was security. During these uncertain times, how could a girl *not* invest in her appearance? Future psychologists would refer to this uptick in cosmetic spending during economic downturns as the "lipstick index"[3] and tie its existence to pressures to survive and mate during lean times. Lipstick was now more than an accessory—it was an economic necessity, a love spell, and a life raft.

In 1938, the *Chicago Daily Tribune* asked readers, "Lives There a Woman Who is Happy without Lipstick?"[4] (Spoiler alert: no, not a one.) As author Antoinette Donnelly would have it, masterfully applied lipstick was positively the key to contentment: "No matter how busy or in what a hurry she may be, she will take time to put on lipstick. It fills her with confidence and a hope that it will add the moist gleam one sees on the lips of a child—the lips of youth." A weird sentiment to be sure, but also an understandable one in a world in which the blush of youthfulness was social currency and a job requirement. The Institute of Women's Professional Relations[5] advised job seekers that employers' "pet peeves" included "too much rouge or lipstick" and "lipstick on teeth." (Also of note: employers, rather like horses, seemed to be easily spooked by "grotesque hats" and "garish or startling colors" so best to avoid them.)

Even as President Franklin Delano Roosevelt was implementing the New Deal in 1933 to combat the nearly 25 percent unemployment[6] rate, Ms. Donnelly was all in on the power of a well-painted face. Massive public works and infrastructure investment were fine and dandy, but where did that leave the plain girl in a sea of laborers? Nowhere, that's where. "Time and again," she warned her *Tribune* readers, "I've been told by employers and employment agencies that a girl's appearance matters more than brains, brawn, fidelity. If a girl isn't smart enough to get herself up cleverly and keep herself so—she's just out of date on modern employment ethics as far as women are concerned, which couples efficiency with personal appearances."[7] The American woman of the 1930s certainly faced some uncharted territory—not only was she working outside of the house in record numbers (by choice or necessity), but she was facing standards of dress and conduct that even her mother's generation had never seen. Moreover, with an increasing number of women in the workforce competing for an extremely limited number of jobs, it was not enough just to wear lipstick; again, one had to be deft in its application or face life on the breadlines—every woman must be a makeup artist in addition to a stenographer, seamstress, and cook, otherwise she is unemployable.

Also in the last few years of the twenties, the manual of domesticity and respectability, *Good Housekeeping*, completely changed its tune about wearing makeup. No longer a barrier to middle-class wholesomeness, now it proclaimed, "Beauty Is Part of Your Job."[8] The magazine's beauty editor, Louise Paine Benjamin (who indeed had beauty in her job title), advised women as they headed out into the workforce that

> Brains and a diploma, ambition and common sense, are all excellent equipment for a job, but these days we don't put up good merchandise in shoddy packages! . . . When you get out your diploma and your references and set out to lay siege to the business world, you should also give some serious consideration to the impression you make physically. Don't rely on personality and the fact that you were an honor student.

The message was clear: whatever a modern woman's ambitions or needs, it was still a man's world, and she better make herself presentable, and—for the love of God—don't let your brains or sparkling personality get in the way of your good looks! Nope. Instead, the right lipstick and careful wardrobing were obligatory, since they tempered or hid any threat posed by female aspirations.

Even First Lady Eleanor Roosevelt was not immune to the obligation to paint and fluff. A slight makeover in 1938 earned breathless column inches in the *Washington Post*. "A flutter of whispered comments up one row and down the other when Mrs. Roosevelt entered the second-floor sitting room where a flock of newspaper women were waiting for the weekly press conference. The First Lady was wearing lipstick—and there was a hint of rouge on her cheeks!"[9] *Lipstick and rouge—exclamation point!* Mrs. Roosevelt, pioneering feminist, labor advocate, and voice for human rights, had succumbed to the pressure to wear makeup at the suggestion of her daughter, Alice. A move that, according to biographer Blanche Wiesen Cook, neither satisfied her particularly (she called it "a great time

& care consumer!") nor the odd religious critic who worried that her brazen example would lead young women astray.[10] Even if Mrs. Roosevelt's look wasn't all the rage among teens (and it's safe to say it wasn't), she did speak to a lot of women in terms of the classic push-pull of domestic obligation versus work outside the home, although her lot was one that included staff and a blue-blood pedigree.

At the other end of the social scale—but under no less pressure to keep up appearances—was Bonnie Parker of "Bonnie and Clyde" fame. Folk heroes of a sort, Bonnie and Clyde's bank-robbing exploits and car chases kept newspaper readers enthralled. A certain segment of the press, eager to cash in on the infamy and any possible affront to womanhood, tracked their scandalous (and unmarried!) tear across the country with breathless attention to Bonnie's outfits, supposed cigar smoking, and alleged gun toting. When Bonnie and Clyde were finally tracked down and killed in a storm of bullets by a posse in Gibsland, Louisiana, on May 23, 1934, the papers were quick to note that among the guns and stolen license plates found in the death car, there was also "A small overnight kit [that] held Bonnie's lipstick, powder, and personal effects."[11] Being on the lam from a virtual army of G-men and local law enforcement was apparently no excuse to let your looks slip. Probably also thanks to the movies, so much glamour still clings to their legend that the makeup case itself (sans lipstick or "personal effects") sold for $12,000 in 2012.

No matter one's station, the financial woes of the Depression still meant the timeless wear and tear of classic expectations of the roles as wife and mother against the financial reality that necessity posed. A 1936 Roper poll found that only 15 percent of Americans believed women should work outside of the home, with another 37 percent conceding conditional approval. Compare this with the fact that 24.3 percent of women over the age of fourteen were working in some capacity, the majority employed in traditionally female roles—domestic service, teachers, nurses, and so forth.[12] And all of them—those with a paycheck, those on the hunt, and those who were still at home—needed to find the right shade of lipstick, but quick. Luckily the beauty industry was in a good position to help.

That was for women workers—and women only. For men, showing up in public in lipstick was almost certainly meant to be a form of humiliation. During a garment workers strike, in particular, it was meant to send a signal. According to a unionist paper of the time, "Quite a furor was caused on 34th Street at Eighth Avenue at 4pm when Pete Feldburg, a 19-year-old scab of 273 Stanton Street, stepped out of a cab naked as the day he was born. A crowd of several thousand gathered and seemed very amused at the young man's nudity and the signs painted all over his body in red lipstick, 'I am a scab'"[13] Management and labor would continue to have their issues (and, in New York especially, their connections with the strange bedfellows of the mob and socialists) throughout the era, but gender lines where not meant to be tampered with. The union was sending a literal signal with poor young Pete's body that everybody in midtown Manhattan could understand. Although, surprisingly enough, not Pete himself. "When asked by a reporter if he would now join the union, Feldburg replied, 'I certainly will not. That's no way to treat a person.'"[14] Perhaps he was willing to risk it, but others certainly took the hint.

While many other American industries were trying to find their feet again, the cosmetics field was flourishing (albeit with some individual hiccups) with an estimated $750 million in sales in 1930.[15] This was a golden age of advertising experimentation with brands using print, radio, celebrity endorsement, aspirational cache, and the promise of romance in search of the magical formula that drove women to the department store counters, drugstores, and salons with their precious dollars. The wizardry, it seemed, was in the promise of beauty itself. One consistent theme that emerged was that lipstick was a sort of lottery ticket, and riches of some kind awaited if you possessed it. This gave the cosmetic advertising of the period a certain Horatio Alger-esque quality to it, suggesting that a change of destiny could be yours with enough luck, pluck, and adept application of the right products.

Another popular source of information about makeup and its proper use was the pamphlet. A loss leader for cosmetic companies, they were given away or sold for a nominal fee through magazines and distributors. These handy little how-to guides advised on useful matters such as the proper method for washing one's face, the right way to rouge, and other life skills you might not have picked up along the way. The pages of "New Loveliness for You," "Beauty in the Making," and "Beauty in the Modern Mode," offered sage advice from bona fide experts like Richard Hudnut, Madame Helena Rubinstein, and Charles of the Ritz, respectively. They were, of course, what we now refer to as advertorials, which means that the success of the methods described therein could be achieved only with purchase of the brands' unique products, but in spirit their real mission was to help you unlock your truly beautiful self, which had long been unfortunately stifled by dull skin, dry elbows, and caked foundation. These booklets further encouraged women to start young, as in the case of "Cosmetics: Their Purpose and Proper Use," which was offered as a supplement to high school home economics teachers. It turns out that Armand cosmetics were proper, since they produced the book and the transformative products within.

Although industry missives were widely available, a more commonly used resource was the steady, staid parade of monthly advice offered by the ladies' magazine category. Long a holdout on the propriety of makeup, magazines had changed with the times, perhaps in no small part to shifting attitudes overall *and* the amount of money makeup advertisers paid to appear in them. Splashed across the pages of *Ladies' Home Journal*, *Good Housekeeping*, *Redbook*, and other publications were the greatest and latest developments in domesticity. Squarely aimed at middle-class women, these magazines employed a strategy that both preyed on women's fears and encouraged them to be their best, most gracious, most female selves. Their friendly (if slightly nosy and bossy) neighborly tone fit right in with the American fantasy of social mobility and propriety: ceaselessly aspirational (without being vulgar), devoted to self-improvement (without being obvious), and on trend (without being shocking).

These secrets to success were yours for the asking, if you were willing to apply yourself, promised the advertisements peppered throughout these periodicals. Angelus Ideal Rouge by Louis Phillipe, for example, offered to teach "How Women of Social Prominence Now Make-Up."[16] Their lipsticks were positively "the right make-up" and never looked "cheap" (read: lower class). Tattoo brand lipstick (so called for its alleged staying power) assured consumers "To Be Correct—Tattoo Your Lips," theirs was "truly exciting color . . . the smartest ever seen!" and for only a dollar.[17] And perhaps most confusingly, Tangee, which promised to deliver male attention but also render it benign: "Women Liked Her . . . But Men Whispered! Now she attracts . . . without attracting attention." The story in the ad lays out the tale of the "girl with the painted lips,"[18] who switched to a more natural lipstick and was rewarded with respectability for a mere thirty-nine cents. It was as if each ad was a tiny soap opera playing out the dramas of class, gender, and mistaken identity.

Between the ads, the editorial pages also devoted oceans of ink to lipstick, its selection, application, and powers. Beauty was possible even for the plain, they assured readers, it was just going to take some work. *Ladies' Home Journal* gently guided readers along with the assertion, "Don't be discouraged if the mirror fails to reveal beauty. Real beauty begins behind your forehead. If you are courageous enough to face your mirror and analyze what you see there, not hopelessly or regretfully, but intelligently, there is no reason you can't manufacture personality." If that seems a little harsh, the author, Grace Mack, follows it up with the reassurance that "There is no doubt that makeup and hairdressing play a most important part in the manufacture of a personality. But these are externals. *True personality comes from within.*"[19] (Emphasis hers.) Mack notes being particularly inspired by the lip lines drawn by Katharine Hepburn to overcome the fact that she was "not beautiful in the standard sense of the word." A fuller, more sensual mouth was the real power behind the talent. It all added to the driving idea that the correct application of lipstick told the world who you were—or, perhaps more importantly, who you wanted to be.

Ruth Murrin at *Good Housekeeping* was also full of advice on "Getting along with Your Own Face."[20] Her basic thesis revolved around the notion that all faces were in some way flawed but, through the magic of lipstick and powders, could be made presentable, even palatable. It was a theme she returned to over and over again, and it was one of obligation: you had to know how to color and camouflage. No excuses! She praised one diligent reader as an example, stating "You're wise to be so careful about your choice of lipstick. . . . Every girl should cultivate a discriminating sense of color. Then she will be able to give full value to her best points—a lovely complexion, bright hair, eyes of an unusual color—an important step for one who wants to be a perennial beauty."[21] The implications were deep: beauty was flighty and fragile; choosing the wrong shade of lipstick could throw your entire life's plans into chaos and leave you stuck at the bottom of the social or financial ladder.

Not all women's magazines were created equal, however. There's a distinct class element to the American fantasy of mass consumption that plays out in the pages of these periodicals. Whereas domestic publications were focused squarely on nonstop striving, improvement, and reputability, fashion magazines assumed readers were well-heeled and worldly enough to know the difference between a chiffon and a chignon. Copy concerned itself less with the scary state of the economy, the drudgery of jobs, and learning social graces and more with the latest, the loveliest, and the most lavish. If you were already at the top, the presumption was you simply knew the proper way to make up, so focus was largely on trend and purchasing as an issue of social form; for example, what to give for Christmas, what to wear on summer vacation, and where to shop for it all. Advice often included finding inspiration in one's jewels or from the other girls at university, all of which breezily assumed that these things were an option during the harshest economic conditions the United States had ever seen. Not that wealthier women were exempt from the work of beauty—they, too, had to examine for flaws and protect against aging; they just had financial wherewithal to do so in a grander manner. "We are all painted ladies to-day," conceded *Vogue*, adding, "It is not a question of whether or not we make up or not, but if we make up well enough."[22]

Even the young were encouraged to work seriously on their levels of cosmetic sophistication. Those rarefied few studying at an advanced level especially didn't want to be left behind in the beauty game—no matter the major, the life of a coed seemed to revolve around grooming and shopping, then, if there was time, studying. "There are, we discovered, mice in college. Mice who haven't changed their hairdo since boarding school. Mice who always buy the same shade of lipstick. Mice who wash their face and just wait for glamour to descend upon them, rather than rolling up their sleeves and doing something about it. Are you a mouse?" No, you are not, was the presumptive answer. Moreover, "Are you timid about modern improvements, as, say, lipstick pencils—or, worse do you think of them in some vague, impersonal way, as you would the war in Spain? Come now. The autumn competition is about to begin."[23] Get it together, girls! Franco's army was on the march, and here you are with unlined lips! Your bunk at, say, Radcliffe may have offered different day-to-day concerns than that of the waitress or secretary, but you were united in your need to mobilize feminine grace and ultimately land and keep a proper husband.

This is not to say that everyone who had a copy of *Vogue* or *Harper's Bazaar* was on the social register. There was then, as there is now, an element of consumer fantasy in those pages. The lure of upward mobility and the promise of purchasing power had to have been incredibly appealing during the dark days of the Depression. All mass media outlets picked up on this need for material escapism in one way or another, but the movies in particular masterfully presented a world replete with black lacquer floors and fur-trimmed satin gowns, a universe where every shopgirl could marry well and for love (usually at the same time), if she were just pretty and plucky enough. Musicals, "women's pictures," and screwball comedies represented forms of window-shopping in the dark. Several movies even paused their plots entirely to host random fashion shows in the first reel, notably *Fashions of 1934*, *Vogues of 1938*, and *The Women* with its color footage and gowns by the fabulous Adrian. There were, of course, affordable alternatives made available to the actual working girl in the form of studio-branded sewing patterns, fan magazines, and celebrity-endorsed complexion soaps.

The rise of celebrity culture with the advent of motion pictures inextricably linked the notion of cosmetics and glamour, partially by necessity, since film lights required cosmetics to make players' features pop, and partly by design, since the movie tie-in would turn out to be as lucrative as the pictures themselves for generations to come. In an era during which women made the bulk of ticket-buying decisions, cheaply produced and widely available fan magazines were targeted straight at that segment of the population. Less opulent than their worldly Condé Nast counterparts, Madame Rubenstein, Elizabeth Arden, and House of Guerlain mostly didn't bother with them. Instead, on their pages you'd find ads for laundry soap, floor polish, and massmarket cosmetic brands (e.g., Tangee, Tattoo, Maybelline) next to articles about the loves, clothes, and careers of Hollywood's brightest stars. Profiles of studio players and starlets were designed to make them both enviable and relatable. For example, you loved the boost of a new lipstick and so did they! "A new lipstick means a new point of view on life to most women and I'm no exception,"[24] exclaimed melodrama star Helen Twelvetrees. The Hollywood fan magazine was a format that allowed you to see yourself in your favorite actress's satin evening slippers.

As for beauty advice, the fan magazines largely followed the same formula as fashion and ladies' publications—be your best self with makeup—but with the addition of famous faces. The writers here were tasked with selling double the fantasy—beauty *and* fame—made possible with transformative powers of makeup. As *Screenland* writer Sydney Valentine put it in 1930 in her article on the "Miracles of Makeup," "The pen may be mightier than the sword, but the lipstick and the eyebrow pencil are mightier than the pen. . . . A few hours in makeup artist's chair, the hairdressers, and the gown designers, and homely girls emerge as beauties and beautiful maidens become breathtaking visions."[25] This was indeed miraculous, and since it made good looks less luck of the genetic draw and more of a function of purchasing power, it created an ache that easily could be remedied. This was an especially important theme during the Depression, when getting consumers to part with their hard-earned nickels for anything other than the essentials of food and housing was more of a challenge. Making beauty attainable in this way put lipstick at the center of a capitalist utopia, where nearly all female consumers had access to its potential.

Max Factor, having already established himself as *the* movie makeup genius, continued to perfect his messaging. His advertising of the era offered to reveal no less than the "Secrets of the Stars" and featured even more women who were happy (and contractually obligated) to share the magical colors and techniques he had given them on their way to success. Contemporary Max Factor copy promised lavishly: "Imagine color tones in face powder, rouge, and lipstick so wonderful as to enhance the beauty of your favorite star. Think of the beauty they will bring to you." This was a generous thought and sold well to a great portion of women but assumed you fit into the same color scheme as Jean Harlow, Joan Crawford, or Claudette Colbert. As ever, for women of color, finding lipsticks that complemented their looks and ideals was a more complicated issue, especially during an era in which beauty was linked to money-making potential.

For Black women in particular, the pressures surrounding appearance were myriad—they shared with white women a fear of aging and a desire to appeal to men—but compounding this was a model of beauty that valued whiteness above all else. In addition to a wider range of powders (Max Factor, for example, stopped at Amber #2), cosmetic companies aimed at the African American community offered bleaching creams and other aids that perpetuated the standard. Meanwhile, in the press, Black-owned papers were careful to tread the line between uplift and conformity. In her column "How to Look Your Best" in the *New York Amsterdam News*,

Hollywood's makeup genius. Max Factor's advertising promised to make movie star glamour achievable, affordable, and essential for every woman but was designed for a limited range of skin tones. *Library of Congress*

writer Fanette advised readers to use lipstick with caution. "Lipstick is decidedly popular. However, it is wise to remember whether it is popular or not, it is better to use too little than too much. A person with large lips should be very careful when wielding the lipstick. When using lipstick remember that you are making your mouth more prominent and use your judgment as to whether you can afford to have more prominent lips."[26] This was a heavy warning to a population that had been hit even harder by the Depression than most.

Again, when beauty was currency, self-improvement was an incredibly important weapon in a woman's arsenal. Columnist Emmita Cardozo viewed makeup as part of an overall pride in appearance that would lead to upward mobility for all.

> Today, more than any time in the history of our race, women are becoming conscious of their personal appearance. It is my sincere wish that the experience I have had in schools of beauty and my studies with "past masters" of the art will help me write just the thing you have been looking for to help improve your personal appearance. . . . Can we not inaugurate our own methods of procedure in our looks without using the hints put in the paper for women of the Caucasian race? By imitating the assets of other women, we are apt to lose sight of our own physical assets.[27]

This view made lipstick more than just good grooming and fun; it was self-determination and confidence in a world that saw you as less beautiful by virtue of your race.

As problematic as white-centered beauty standards were (and remain), the world of beauty culture itself was one of the few places where minority women could experience financial success on par with any white titan of industry. Madame C. J. Walker, Madame Sarah Spencer Washington, and Annie Malone were among the nation's first self-made female millionaires, and they all made their fortunes in hairdressing and cosmetics by Black women for Black women. However, not all companies that catered to women of color were Black owned. Valmor was founded in 1926 by Morton and Rose Neumann, a Jewish couple from Chicago, who would—like Madame Rubinstein—invest their substantial profits into a notable modern art collection. At a time when salons like Madame Rubinstein's and Arden's Red Door would not even admit women of color through the front door, these entrepreneurs were serving their communities and raking in cash, much of which they reinvested in philanthropy and other Black-owned businesses.

Moreover, the beauty business provided much-needed jobs. So much so that the New Deal's Federal Writers' Project studied the density and stratification of the 161 beauty parlors in Harlem, which ranged from fifteen-cent, straight-comb services to elaborate townhouses dedicated to the cosmetic needs of the area's upper crust.[28] For others in search of opportunities, Lucky Heart Cosmetics provided a door-to-door sales model in the style of Avon. Counter girl positions, factory jobs, and other support roles were also available. Although the industry itself didn't actively encourage diversity, it seemed to tolerate it more than others; perhaps because of the inherent outsider nature of women in business or perhaps just for profit, cosmetics was, and would remain, a space for some savvy outsiders.

In addition to managing its wild growth, the industry as a whole was about to face some serious changes from within and without. In 1936, in what was perhaps an attempt to stave off regulation by the government, an industry group agreed to have its manufacturing methods reviewed by scientists for purity and safety, while another committee would vet advertising for overreaching promises. In practice, it agreed "To review the advertising copy and labels submitted by the industry and to examine such copy in the light of the dictates of good taste and in conformity contained in the Federal Trade Commission stipulations."[29] Presumably "loveliness," "prominent social standing," and "perfect daintiness" made the grade, because they remained advertising buzz words throughout the decade.

Self-regulation seemed only to postpone the inevitable, and in 1938 Congress passed the Federal Food, Drug, and Cosmetic Act. The fears posed by an unchecked industry turned out not to be unfounded. Before passage of the act, several consumers had been blinded by eyelash dyes, and afterward, the government made a huge show of confiscating a massive shipment of "poisonous lipstick!"[30] The deadly cosmetics were imported from France and contained a dose of the toxin selenium. Although the act meant healthier products in the long run, there were concerns about what the changes and consumer skittishness could mean to the lipstick brands and their workers. Industry spokesman Edward Plaut suggested that fewer small manufacturers could now enter the field due to the burden of legislation and indicated that it added to companies' already heavy workload by ensuring that "more women customers will ask questions, and that manufacturers will assume responsibility for educating their salesgirls."[31] Annoying as that might be, it was the cost of doing business and the law was the law; moreover, the industry had agreed to comply. What it could not control was what was going on in the world at large.

The shadow of fascism had long been darkening the horizon of Europe, and although Americans had kept the troubles abroad at arm's length for quite some time, certain realities inevitably would cross the Atlantic. Part of the trouble would begin with the autocrats themselves; both Hitler and Mussolini had rallied against beauty and fashion as the enemy of their idealized proletariat states. To the American gal, steeped in a lifetime of capitalism and style, it may have seemed downright laughable and perhaps even a little quaint—and their European counterparts were hard to convince as well. Mussolini's push to compel the women of Italy to forgo imported glamour met with mixed success, to which he conceded, "fashion is more powerful than dictators."[32] The Third Reich was less forgiving. The governor of the Franconia region, Julius Streicher, publicly declared his very specific hatred for Jews, Czechs, and lipstick, telling a gathering of Nazi youth that Aryans were "beautiful, godlike, and natural" and that "Women who use lipstick had better not come here."[33]

Indeed, Hitler himself thought lipstick was suitable only for undesirables such as prostitutes, foreigners, and Jews and encouraged women to go without. In addition to setting the Aryan ideal of beauty, there was likely an economic element to the crackdown. Inflation and economic stagnation plagued the Reich, so much so that the brownshirts took the opportunity to reassign workers from cosmetic manufacturing during a labor shortage, declaring the industry as a whole a "humbug" and admonishing women, "There is no need for 200 various kinds of face creams. Ten are sufficient."[34] Why ten was the reasonable magic number is lost to history.

None of this had significant impact on American appetites for new cases and colors—until it did. The September 1, 1939, invasion of Poland by Germany would plunge the continent of Europe into war and create complications in growing markets, supply chains, and other vulnerable filaments that kept this worldwide industry woven together. The impact already was felt in Britain, where the publisher of *Business Week* feared for the morale of workers, "if their supplies of lipstick and lingerie were diminished."[35] Around the same time, Parisian designers tried to keep things light by designing handbags that could hold both first aid kits and lipstick for the fashion-conscious women facing the threat of air raids.[36] In the United States, isolationism meant that women could still concern themselves with the spring shades: "clear" reds, pink clover, and Burma Ruby.

As Europe was tumbling into the jagged abyss of war, America was effortlessly gliding into a push-button future of robots and television—if not the entire nation, at least the Flushing section of Queens, New York, where the 1939 World's Fair was held. The vast exhibition had been conceived and executed to present Depression-weary visitors with a vision of the "Dawn of a New Era." Beauty was, of course, a part of this shining new world. Located in the section of the park feting American industry, the beauty pavilion was originally dubbed "Vanity Fair" and conceived as a great hall showcasing multiple brands. As opening day approached, however, pressures from the troubled economy forced out all but the mass market brand Coty. Now rechristened "Maison Coty," it was shaped by its architect, Donald Deskey (of Radio City Music Hall fame), to resemble a giant powder box, an art deco temple to femininity. Its interior was filled with lavish stations decorated in the "modern baroque" style of interior designer Dorothy Draper, who devoted every square foot to the art and craft of the manufacturing and deft application of powders, perfumes, and lipsticks. On April 30, 1939, the doors of the "Charm Center of the World's Fair" swung open and offered some twenty-five million visitors an education and shopping opportunity in the nonstop pursuit of loveliness.

Founded by French perfumer François Coty (né Joseph Marie François Spoturno) in 1904, the Coty company would bring the cachet of French cosmetics to the affordable American market by importing the raw materials from France and manufacturing in the United States, thereby avoiding sizable import taxes. Nowhere as exclusive as Elizabeth Arden shades nor as cheap as Tangee lipsticks (which retailed in a thirty-nine-cent size), Coty's Sub-Deb colors hit the middle-class sweet spot with a $1.10 price tag and an aspirational image. Even the name itself (short for subdebutante—that is, a young woman who has not yet made her debut in society) suggested the privileges of youth and entrée into high society, thereby providing women with a necessary luxury and a sure ticket to romance. The Sub-Deb ad copy cooed, "A lipstick, we submit, has one purpose in its brief and vivid life: to make a lady's lips a little more alluring." Accompanying illustrations conceived of their customer as posh, slim, unflaggingly white, and perpetually dressed for society luncheons and supper clubs. In a year where breadlines were still the norm, Coty was selling the consumer fantasy that had long surrounded cosmetics—and selling it hard. It was a fragile bubble dance of an image, one that was about to burst in the most spectacular fashion.

In 1940, about halfway through the Fair, the World of Tomorrow had begun to lose exhibitors who found it necessary to go home to Europe and join the war effort—and some of those who were left behind, like those from newly occupied Poland and Czechoslovakia, for example, didn't have much to celebrate. With the European fashion capitals on virtual lockdown, America would start to look to Latin America for color inspiration; Maison Coty made do by cosponsoring a hat fashion show with milliner Lilly Daché and that featured "deep-keyed colors"[37] inspired by those "exotic" countries of Latin America that still had shipping lanes open under Franklin Roosevelt's "Good Neighbor Policy."

Whatever the prevailing trends in the Americas, by October 1940, it was time to pack up the pavilions and head home. America would stand at the edge of the war for another fourteen months, observing from a distance and enjoying the fruits of its own labor. But December 7, 1941, would, of course, change all of that, and the United States would be forced to send the "boys" and—to an unprecedented extent—the "girls" off to war. As the years of the war unfolded, Americans would rise to the challenge it placed on our resources and our shared values. The Depression was one thing, but war was quite another, and with our sisters around the world increasingly under the shadow of its ugliness (if not already embroiled in it), beauty would have to put its boots on and strap in for the duration.

CHAPTER SIX

BEAUTY IS YOUR DUTY
World War II

Shades of the Decade
Tussy Jeep Red
Elizabeth Arden Montezuma Red
DuBarry Emblem Red
Tangee Natural—"The Uniform Lipstick"
Helena Rubinstein Regimental Red

From the outset of World War II, one thing was clear: loose lips may sink ships, but unpainted ones were a serious threat to the war effort. Lipstick would have to shape up *and* ship out. Even before the first bombs struck Pearl Harbor, beauty culture was anticipating its role in the war effort. It had, after all, been there before. An article by *Washington Post* writer Carolyn Abbott titled "War Promotes Cosmetics' Use, Beautician Says" touted the idea that as veterans of the Great War, lipsticks, powders, and paints would be there to serve in the next fight. According to Mrs. Margaret Argeter, an industry expert quoted in the article, "During the wars men wave the flags and women the lipsticks. Ever beauty conscious, the female becomes even more so during wars. And regardless of how hard pressed economically the country becomes, women will continue to use make-up in some form,"[1] adding that the number of beauty parlors had exploded during the intervening years from a mere 1,000 in 1914 to more than 84,000 in 1941, now including every state in the union.

Being abreast of the latest trends was as necessary a female-linked skill as typing or homemaking or, as the article put it, "the modern woman is learning to apply make-up adeptly." More than just good grooming, lipstick and powder were a necessity, a totem of femininity, and the mark of modernity itself. Beauty was marching forward—regardless of what the Axis powers would throw in its way.

As *Saturday Evening Post* writer J. C. Furnas put it in a 1941 article entitled "Glamour Goes to War," "Queer things would naturally happen when the American woman's instinct to be beautiful collides with a thoughtless world's insistence on fighting a war."[2] Namely, supply line interruptions of European cosmetic imports and ingredients and the armed forces' need for material support in the form of metals, emollients, and petroleum derivatives, which made up the basis of lipsticks, would soon prove to be serious challenges to long-established values and the easy access to consumer goods that Americans had known even in the depths of the Depression. Contingency plans would have to be made for America's place in the beauty world. Doing without silk stockings and fresh vegetables for the good of our troops fighting abroad was one thing; aesthetic austerity from a lack of cosmetics at home was quite another. The solution, it seemed, was to adapt to the times—rationing, shortages, and workloads be damned, the American woman would keep up her appearance—along with the home fires—through innovation. Lipstick, one of the most desired, most recognized morale boosters, would lead the charge in several forms: as an unofficial support team, as part of the women's uniform, both in service and at home, and as a brilliantly effective "us versus them" form of propaganda.

With the formal declaration of war by Congress in December 1941, America wasn't just *at* war, it was in the *business* of war. The entire globe was now involved, and in addition to recovering from major economic setbacks, organizing this worldwide effort would take some doing, materials shuffled around, sacrifices made. Lipstick was facing a particularly tough slog thanks to the most basic ingredients that made its existence possible. The formula for lipstick consisted of a wax base combined with varying levels of emulsifiers (usually an oil) and dyes melted together, which was poured into a mold to cool with the final, projectile-shaped product placed in a metal tube. As a result of the conflicts worldwide, the various raw ingredients became harder to come by: lanolin and mineral oils had come from as far afield as Australia, Brazil, and Cuba and the wax from Ethiopia. Some could be resourced domestically or from Latin America, and some, like the metal for cases, could be replaced entirely by new materials, such as cardboard or plastic. The new tube also freed up metal for much-needed bullets. It was all a shift and a pinch, but the essential red pout would endure.

The Associated Press broke the news of rationing to America's women in July 1942, explaining that "In the war's greatest blow to boudoir and bathroom, the War Production Board (WPB) established manufacturing limits on beauty preparations, estimating the restriction would save some 17,400,000 pounds of chemicals and other critical war materials annually."[3] The WPB was tasked with ensuring that the nation had everything it needed to fight the enemy from bootlaces to bombs, and it had decreed that precious glycerin, packaging materials, and other elements of lipstick production would have to be conserved so that the bulk of these items could go to the military. It was a sacrifice, but one of national pride—our enemies could slow down production, but they couldn't kill consumers' appetites for beauty. Articles like (the incredibly, sadly emblematic of its era) "Lipstick Containers Can Fight the Japs"[4] encouraged women to throw their metal tubes in with the rest of the scrap metals being collected for munitions—a small but mighty gesture, considering American women consumed some sixty-five million tubes of the stuff annually.

Within the industry, even the setbacks of rationing and manufacturing limits would soon be turned into public relations positives. An anonymous industry advertisement began appearing in *Cosmopolitan* to drive home the point that it's "Patriotic to Be Pretty" and laying out all the hard work that cosmetics manufacturers were doing to keep the economy humming on the home front and the positive virtues of maintaining your makeup routine.[5] Even small gestures were newsworthy—Max Factor let consumers know that it was in on the scrap frenzy by donating its used rubber, namely the "mechanical kissing" lips it used to test its lipstick's staying power.[6] Everyone from the CEO to the shopgirl was in it together, and beauty brands were determined to prove their patriotic mettle. Brass would be saved, bonds sold, new forms of hard work touted in ads:

- Along with new colors, Tangee advocated "Beauty—glory of woman . . . Freedom—glory of nations . . . protect them both . . . buy war savings certificates."

- The Barbara Gould brand reminded women that "Metal for lipstick cases is restricted, and soon there will be no more containers. It is patriotic as well as economical to save your present lipstick cases and buy refills."

- And Revlon recognized that women were leading a "double life": "number one, the busy war worker; number two, charming companion to your man," and that these demands required matching lip and nail colors.

All of which—the work, the war, and the national fervor—were new territories both for consumers and companies to explore.

The early years of the war would mark some interesting changes in marketing and consumption in response to the seismic shifts occurring in women's roles that distinguished America's war effort in this conflict from previous campaigns. With the armed forces growing by the day, women would take on duties they had never been offered before, namely in uniforms and on assembly lines, and adjustments to the way beauty was sold and bought would have to be made. What did femininity mean if you handled a rivet gun? Was it silly to worry about your lipstick when our boys were away fighting? Why even make up at all? The answers came quickly and resoundingly. Appearances needed to be maintained and things would go back to normal eventually. Just a couple months into the war, the *Los Angeles Times* touted the idea that "Feminine Role in National Defense Starts at Beauty Shop," adding that one young, anonymous, volunteer officer said that he wanted to go off to the front knowing that he could "come back from this war to find my girl as pretty as I left."[7] And looking that pretty, as every American girl knew, took some ammunition of her own.

Wherever you went, lipstick was there. It had to be—it was the American way. At least for some Americans, but for Americans of color, the war experience was vastly different. Blacks would serve in segregated units; Latinx Americans would continue to face discrimination and police violence at home, and, in general, nonwhite Americans would be asked to do their part for their country while being excluded from many of its privileges. For many Japanese Americans, the war years were less an exercise in love of country and more a nightmare of betrayal and institutionalized racism made tangible. With Executive Order 9066, President Roosevelt upended the lives of over one hundred thousand U.S. citizens by ordering them to be rounded up and placed in internment camps throughout the American West. Although Italian Americans and German Americans (even the thousands who had previously pledged allegiance to the motherland in the form of the pro-Nazi German American Bund before the war) remained undisturbed, Japanese Americans were summarily stripped of their rights and forced to leave behind their homes, businesses, and communities, only to be resettled in prisonlike camps far from everything they knew.

Despite challenging conditions, high spirits and good looks had to be maintained by the women of Manzanar. Located in the foothills of the Sierra Nevada in California, the camp was home to ten thousand men, women, and children. Facilities included schools, gardens, and a general store with everything inmates might need. According to its newsletter, the ironically titled *Manzanar Free Press*, "To keep up with the latest vogue and beauty make-ups; the ladies are trotting down to the local dry goods

Beauty is your duty. A teenage internment camp inmate circa World War II. A Japanese-American woman keeps up appearances for the war effort. *Ansel Adams, Library of Congress.*

store. Mazanettes haunt the cosmetics department daily. . . . To match the ladies' now tanned complexions, darker shades of lipstick and powder are in great demand. The bright ladies decide to take home the matching rouge and lipstick." Even to these women, who found themselves in circumstances that strained their identity and their place in American life, it seems that the morale boost and normalcy of lipstick was being touted as an important obligation for the duration.

The Allies—America in particular—had cast their lot on the side of team lipstick with a fervor that matched any stripe of patriotism. In addition to lifting spirits, maintaining a sense of traditional gender roles, and fueling the free market, beauty was freedom almost in a literal sense. By this time, Americans were well aware that makeup had been a longtime target of fascism. At first it was almost laughable, spawning headlines like "Nazis Impose Dowdiness"[8] and "Homemaking under Hitler,"[9] which snarked about the Reich's strange little domestic regulations. Makeup itself was verboten in the Third Reich, with Hitler and Goebbels going so far as to ban women who were wearing makeup from attending the Nazi women's auxiliary, the NSBO. Not that some fascists didn't flirt with the trappings of glamour. In 1937, Mussolini's own son, aspiring filmmaker Vittorio Mussolini, would make a trip to Hollywood to study various movie techniques and observe Max Factor expertly dab the young starlet Betty Grable with the latest in film-tested cosmetics.[10] With the war in full swing, however, it was time to draw lines, and clearly American gumption and good looks always would win out over sad sack, bare-faced Aryan fräuleins or the equally dull, colorless companions of Italy's fascist blackshirts.

Besides which, our sisters under the blitz had it much worse: wartime austerity had left them with few ways to paint a "stiff upper lip." With the fall of France in spring 1942, the widespread damage done to Britain due to German bombs, and the general grind of supply shortages, the women of the United Kingdom found themselves scrambling for even the most basic of beauty supplies. More than a blow to self-esteem, this loss was considered an offense to the nation's esprit de corps. According to reporters on the ground, the need was felt particularly acutely by a nation of malnourished women who had abandoned their traditional roles and were putting their all into the war effort. "The main cry of women is that they work harder than ever before and get less fresh air and healthful food and therefore must have the minimum of make-up to compensate for the wear and tear of the hard struggle of daily existence."[11] The English rose would prove to be as resourceful as she was strong, coming up with substitutes like beet juice standing in as a lip stain when things got truly desperate. Additionally, her American beauty counterpart would do what she could to help by sending care packages of toiletries and cosmetics to Britain in a gesture of international goodwill via charities like the British War Relief Society.[12]

On the American home front, things were moving rapidly, and citizens were adjusting to the changes, chief among them being the need for labor. All able-bodied men were needed to fight, which meant that factories, construction, civil service jobs, and other traditionally male roles would have to rely on female workers for the first time. Although the Depression had seen record numbers of women working outside the home, those jobs were largely the sort of pink-collar jobs that had always gone to women; for example, clerical, nursing, teaching, or domestic service, such as housekeepers, cooks, and child care. It's not that women hadn't been in factories; they certainly had been laboring in the mills and sewing in sweatshops since the Industrial Revolution but being on the heavy-machinery assembly lines of the 1940s was different enough in form and function that it upset the delicate balance of gender norms. This switch to women in blue-collar jobs historically controlled by men added yet another scary element to already uncertain times. During an era in which most women didn't own pants, these newfound economic and professional freedoms would be an adjustment for everyone, regardless of race or class. Author Lula Garrett, writing in her weekly column "Lipstick" in the *Baltimore Afro-American*, assured concerned readers, "Some of the elders are worried about the girls losing their femininity in the era of overalls and riveting machines. But there is little need to become excited. As long as girls have enough of Eve in them to put on lipstick and men have enough curiosity to find out what is underneath the lipstick, the future of the human race is safe."[13]

Makeup would help make that transition easier. Though not at all necessary for work in a practical sense, it reassured everyone involved that women could maintain, for better or worse, some semblance of the status quo. The factory floor was apparently no place to forget you were in a man's world—looks mattered, no matter how demanding the job. "You can see how this feminine army of war workers must revolutionize their former method of beauty care," said the *Baltimore Sun*. "In coping with these problems, the girls must remember that the trim, well-turned-out woman is spotted first for the factory job, and then her ability as a skilled worker is determined."[14] It was estimated that by 1943 some six million women would be working in factories, and though rules and regulations varied, they allowed, if not encouraged, these novel new workers to bring some elements of their beauty routine with them. Bans were occasionally enforced, but then it was for health and safety reasons and not a sense of job equity. Lipstick was, for example, forbidden on welders because it could trap dust from metal filings and cause lead poisoning. In at least one case, the excess displays of femininity were bad for production, when, in a charming malfunction of amateur morale building, a batch of munitions had to be scrapped when it was found to be stained with red dye that might foul the ammunition. Upon further inspection, it was revealed that the marks were lipstick placed by patriotic factory girls who had sealed them with a kiss for their sweethearts overseas. "'Save the kisses,' plant officials said."[15] For similar reasons (it smeared addresses and rendered envelopes semitransparent), the post office requested the same protocol for the mail sent to soldiers.

Of course, not all work was done on the assembly line. A number of women also handled civil service jobs that needed to be filled. For them, positions of authority had to be tempered with the expected level of femininity, too. New York City's female police officers were issued leather bags that held both a .38-caliber service revolver and a lipstick,[16] whereas the "lady conductors" of Washington, D.C., had detachable pouches on their belts that were specifically designed to keep both their makeup and transfers in good order.[17]

Along with their work in production and patrols, women would answer Uncle Sam's call in record numbers. Although women around the armed forces wasn't a new phenomenon, either—they had nursed, clerked, laundered, camp followed, and otherwise supported the men since the war for independence—this was a different kind of war, and it would provide women with new opportunities. In addition to existing nursing programs, uniformed nongovernmental organization support groups such as the USO, Red Cross, and Civil War Patrol, each branch of the military would add an auxiliary corps specifically for women.

The army had the Women's Army Auxiliary Corps or WAACs (the word "auxiliary" would be dropped, so just WACs after 1943); the navy welcomed the Women Accepted for Voluntary Emergency Service (or WAVES, get it?!); female flyers enlisted with the Women's Airforce Service Pilots (WASPs); Marine Corps had its Women's Reserve (officially, no cool nickname; unofficially, BAMs, or Broad Ass Marines); and the Coast Guard had the SPARs (which wasn't exactly an acronym, but the first letters of the Latin motto, *semper paratus*, or "always ready"). All told, some 350,000 American women would serve their country, and although they were expressly forbidden from combat (WAVES, SPARs, and Marines weren't even allowed overseas for most of the fight), they'd fill roles at nearly every other level of the war machine. Like their brothers in arms, they would naturally have to be outfitted, equipped, and trained—the difference being that women would be expected to maintain a sense of glamour throughout even the darkest hours of the conflict.

Uniforms and the accompanying accoutrements would be adjusted for a new generation. If lipstick was more of a rarity for their mothers and grandmothers during World War I, it was clearly now so much a part of public appearance that it would have to receive official approval. Head of the WAACs and their "feminine West Point" in West Des Moines, Iowa, Major Mrs. William P. Hobby (née Oveta Culp) had pressing questions waiting for her at Roosevelt's announcement of the creation of the program, and, not surprisingly, they followed a decidedly stereotypical line of inquiry: "There are a great many details in setting up the corps to be worked out—is lipstick essential to feminine morale? What should the correct military skirt length be? What constitutes 'AWOL' for a WAAC?"[18] Turns out that the answer to the first question was a resounding *yes*. "History may record that World War II reached some kind of a turning point today—for Uncle Sam's nieces have taken up the job of helping America on to victory . . . and the archives of the Army hold no previous reports showing that the chief of staff and his assistant sat down to a press conference in which the questions were: Can a WAAC wear lipstick—colored nail polish? They'll be allowed to use them if they're inconspicuous."[19] What constituted "inconspicuous" would presumably be left to enlistees and their commanders, but generally this still allowed for the omnipresent red lips.

One of the things military women shared with their male counter-parts was that the exactingly regimented days did not leave much time for primping. Beauty routines couldn't be abandoned, but they did have to be streamlined. For this task, the defense department brought in the big guns—Madame Helena Rubinstein. Mme. Rubinstein had seen the enemy and it was frumpiness: "Good grooming will be more important than ever. For a woman draws her courage, her hope, and her strength from her knowledge that she is attractive and well-groomed." Toward this end, she developed a number of routines that ranged in commitment from one to fifteen minutes and dictated color palettes. "Mme. Rubinstein thinks a clear, vibrant red accents the various colored defense uniforms to best advantage."[20]

Beyond just a trend, shades of red lipstick would come to be emblematic of the whole era's aesthetic. From the healthy blush of Rosie the Riveter's determined mouth to the cherry cheesecake smiles of Gil Elvgren's pinup girls, the red, almond-shaped mouth now serves as a visual shorthand for the entirety of that moment's sense of fashion and femininity. It was sex appeal paired with national pride in a spectrum of scarlet shades that added new verve to the red, white, and blue. Even the names of colors were mobilized for the fight: Fighting Red by Tussy, Victory Red by Elizabeth Arden, Regimental Red by Helena Rubinstein, Lentheric's Rocket Red, Louis Philippe's Patriot Red, DuBarry's Emblem Red, and dozens more. It was patriotism you could carry in your purse, and women wanted it.

Lipsticks and other cosmetics were popular gifts for women in uniform. Their presence in their lives and their lockers stood as a source of comfort and a reminder of home. They were also one of their most coveted luxuries. Companies sold premade kits with harmonized tones of lipstick, rouge, nail polish, and other "dainties" that made shopping and mailing easier than sending the proverbial "salami to your boy in the army." Surveys were taken to determine the best way to pamper our girls in uniform, and although it varied from branch to branch (slippers, wristwatches, and housecoats were also popular), lipstick and polish in matching red shades were always at the top of their wish lists. Season after season, it was suggested that women away from home, whether on base or abroad, could always use a new lipstick. Christmas was, of course, a good time to send a beauty gift. Reporter turned lieutenant Bess Stephenson advised on holiday shopping for the military gal in your life: "Buy her the rarest and costliest cologne in your budget and buy her a red lipstick. Surprised? You shouldn't be. WACs are still women and some of them have been in uniform for more than a year now."[21]

How could women do without the frills and the paint? It was who they were now, so much so that the word *lipstick* meant womanhood: the Red Cross's jeep unit with its lady drivers was known simply as "the Lipstick Corps."[22] Even the writing about women's competence at work and war would remain something of a novelty in the media and was bound to their makeup, both literally and figuratively. Exemplary of this is a 1942 *New York Times* article with the headline "Women Aim Rifles Handily as Lipstick," which detailed new female recruits' shooting abilities with slightly more enthusiasm than their prepping for the cameras.[23] Lipstick was now firmly part of the uniform of the armed forces, but it also was linked inextricably to the uniform of femininity itself.

Mass media, in the form of magazines and their advertisers, was keenly aware of this shift in mores and was now speaking straight to it. Cosmetic advertising in particular saw a whole new world of possibilities in female recruits. Much like the way vast swaths of today's advertisers speak to the working mom in a way that's empathetic and empowering to her busy lifestyle and the need to treat herself, the industry went all in on the war worker and her unique needs.

- The Barbara Gould brand suggested that women "Take a Beauty Shortcut for Your New Way of Life," whether that was homemaker, factory worker, or enlisted woman.

- "One woman can shorten the war! You're that woman. Yes, you," insisted DuBarry to women doing war work that freed the men to fight.

- Tangee simply cut to the chase in an ad entitled "War, Women, and Lipstick," in which founder Constance Luft Huhn acknowledged, "It's a reflection of the free democratic way of life that you have managed to keep your femininity— even though you are doing a man's work! If a symbol were needed of this fine independent spirit—of this courage and strength—I would choose a lipstick."

Whether the high-minded claims were true or not, what these ads contained was propaganda. It was feminism (for its era), capitalism, comfort, normalcy, fantasy, and so much more at a time in which the world was a scary place and women were uncertain about where they belonged in it. Although some companies were still selling the old standbys of youth, beauty, and romance, by acknowledging women's work, these brands were presaging the future of the cosmetics industry and its consumers—namely, that beauty was the quickest way to a more empowered, more efficient you.

Even before the war wound down entirely, lipstick production was mounting a comeback. In June 1944, the *New York Times* announced, "Lipsticks Better Than in a Long Time."[24] The WPB had released larger supplies of glycerin, and that meant the supply would be smoother and glossier than it had been in a couple of years. To add to that joy, cosmetic cases were also returning to their former glory with manufacturers gaining access to new supplies of carbon steel for their designs. Indeed, the future looked bright for lipstick packaging thanks to the wonders of science. By August of the same year, the *Times* was excited about the possibility of lighter aluminum tubes, because "it is thought that women now prefer the lighter weight of present paper and plastic cases."[25] This change would have to wait until manufacturers could retool in the calm of peacetime, but other than that, sky was the limit.

What did the future hold for those who wore lipstick in years that would follow? The path was less clear on those broader social advancements for those women who had spent the war working, fighting, and otherwise supporting the right side of history. The main question was how women would readjust to a life of profound femininity now that they had a taste of the sort of freedom men had enjoyed for generations. For the beauty press, the change back was offered up as a welcome relief. In a 1946 *Vogue* article entitled "Back on the Pedestal, Ladies," author Barbara Heggie suggested it was time to return to being girly. "In an effort to keep pace with the courage and heroism of their men, women stepped from their pedestal and stripped off their femininity like a soiled wrapper. It was a noble sacrifice, I told myself, but pedestals are rarely vacant for long and now that peace was here again and the ladies were preparing to re-ascend, it was quite a shock to find their place usurped by a pair of trousers."[26] This wouldn't do—the American way was that women were women and men were men, and even if we strayed from that ideal for some global conflict, we could return to it again.

No, at this point, lipstick was practically a requirement for citizenship. Even war brides would come to know this. To make the transition of the one hundred thousand British brides into the exotic traditions of the States as smooth as possible, *Good Housekeeping* offered a booklet entitled *A War Bride's Guide to the U.S.A.*, which advised them that when meeting their in-laws, "remember that in all but the smallest villages, lipstick is expected,"[27] which they presumably could have picked up from our earlier care packages, but better to be sure. This was an important issue of international relations, even if on a small scale.

So the message went out to every American woman, born, naturalized, or just passing through, Lady Liberty might have held her brass-fitted lipstick case "by the Golden Door." Lipstick outlined who we were and who we wanted to be. *Cosmopolitan* defined "the American Girl," as "scrubbed of face, strong of soul. . . . [S]he is wise cracking, casual, warm-hearted, brave. She is a Navy nurse putting on lipstick by the noisy light of shellfire. She is a weary soldier's dream of home."[28] Lipstick would emerge from World War II as a true American victory. In challenging its supply, the Axis powers had challenged everything we held dear: glamour, consumerism, abundance, and innovation. By beating the Axis powers back, we reclaimed it all and spread a powerful message globally. Perhaps not on the same worldwide level as peace, freedom, and prosperity, but it was still emblematic in a micro sense. We were about to enter a moment in American cultural history that would seek to define womanhood in some of the most corseted terms ever, but in the meantime, the luxury and identity of lipstick as part of the female experience had emerged triumphant and resplendent from the haze of war. The coming culture clash of the Cold War and the new model bombshells of the atomic era would throw this success into even starker contrast and spread its all-encompassing message of female capital even further.

CHAPTER SEVEN

THE RED MENACE
The 1950s

Shades of the Decade
Elizabeth Arden Surprise
Dorothy Gray Sea Coral
Revlon Fire and Ice
Hazel Bishop Pink Minx
Sweet Georgia Brown Teezem Red

In 1948, Danish exchange student Merete Bjorn Hanssen tried explaining to her classmates and a local reporter the difference between the democratic socialism of her home country and the communism of the Soviet bloc—it didn't exactly sink in. However, the local reporter did note that she had taken to a more American style of makeup during her stay in the States, "Gobs of lipstick, pancake makeup, and mascara don't appeal to Merete in the least." The reporter noticed an attractive blush-pink color on her cheeks and her faintly tinted lips. "'I suppose it's natural color,' she smiled, 'I did put on a bit of lipstick before school though.' It was then nearly half a day later."[1] Aha! The cultural exchange was complete: she would go home with some cosmetics and Americans would avoid universal health care and pre-K. Not a huge moment in international relations, but one that summarizes the era in many ways. With World War II fought and won, America would experience both peace and prosperity and the Cold War, which would pit everything capitalism had to offer against the threats (real and perceived) of communism.

Lipstick would again find itself enlisted as an emblem and ally of the old red, white, and blue in its fight and would become even more central to American women of every race, class, and creed's sense of self.

The bombs had barely stopped falling when the exports began. There was, of course, the need to rebuild and revitalize the cities and infrastructure that were destroyed by Axis and Allied bombing. While we were at it, it couldn't hurt to build goodwill and consumer demand among countries that had been devastated by the war. Money, industrial support, and construction in the form of the Marshall Plan would go a long way toward getting old and new friends back on their feet, hopefully eliminating the sort of humiliating conditions that helped the Third Reich rise from the Weimar Republic and hemming in the Soviet Union's westward European ambitions. Plus, if they developed a taste for Cadillacs and Max Factor—well, where's the harm? Not that everyone was initially on board with the idea; giving away money to fight communism seemed a bit socialist in more conservative corners, but eventually international goodwill (and long-term strategy) won out. In implementing the plan, there was also a lot of fuss over what constituted aid. "The Question before the House Appropriations Committee: Is Lipstick Essential to Europe" read one article. "The Republican committee members say No. The administration says Yes." GOP Representative Karl Stefan of Nebraska harumphed that "Committee leaders don't feel these are vital in our efforts to strengthen Europe's economy."[2] Mr. Stefan was overruled but grumbling about sending lipstick abroad would continue.

"The Marshall Plan is choking itself to death on nylons, lipstick, plastic combs, and canned tuna fish, Nicholas Farmakis, a Greek student at Bryant College in Providence, RI charges." His objections weren't unfounded; he wanted to see more raw materials and fewer premade goods so that domestic industries could do the manufacturing themselves. Moreover, he argued that the Continent's poor women didn't need those items as a matter of life and death. "Lipsticks and nylons do a lot for American girls, said Farmakis, who is a student of more than business administration, but their use among persons who are supposed to be helped by the Marshall Plan was slight in Greece."[3] America may have been putting the cart in front of the horse in terms of those little luxuries, but our manufacturers were not about to let potential new markets slip through their fingers. Besides, it wasn't like everything was smooth sailing at home either. Even the cosmetics business was adjusting to the demands of the new economy.

According to the head of Coty, Grover Whelan, there was some adjustment in the labor market and the level of demand after the war, which provided a little bump in the road. "Explained Whalen to his stockholders: 'Prices of labor and practically all items entering into our production were sharply advanced. Unfortunately, our industry had no backlog of demand, but quite to the contrary there was already in November 1946, an abundance of supply.'"[4] The solution, at least in part, was to create new demand by creating a new set of consumers. As Europe continued its recovery, industry leaders also turned their attentions to a growing subset of female consumers: the teenager. Adolescents had, of course, been around forever, but with changing mores around lipstick, a growing middle class, and an expanding population of young people, American businesses quickly discovered that bobby-soxers had quite a bit of pocket change and no small amount of angst about their looks and social graces, thereby making them an ideal market. This awareness of their buying power also ushered in a new era of editorial and advertising language that spoke directly to them rather than their parents.

Now that their mothers and possibly grandmothers wore lipstick, the central question was not if one could wear it, but when it was appropriate to start. *Seventeen*, in particular, was a font of information for girls and young women who were too savvy for *Highlights for Children* but not yet sophisticated enough or financially ready for the pages of *Vogue* or *Cosmopolitan* or for the domestic responsibilities of *Ladies' Home Journal* or *Redbook*. Founded in 1944, the content and advertising in the pages of *Seventeen* was generally dictated by the things that have concerned generations of straight, white working- and middle-class teen girls: boys, clear skin, dating, makeup, fashion, boys, career choices, boys, diet, popularity, and pop culture. Lipstick and its use was naturally a perennial favorite.

When it came to its application, *Seventeen* did not hem and haw; it was a necessity and a rite of passage. "Lipstick makes you prettier," it declared in a 1951 article entitled "Learn How."

> To use it is the prerogative of that most wonderful of all creatures . . . a Girl. So, your first lipstick is a genuine event. . . . It is a sign of your coming of age . . . the age at which you become a Girl in earnest.

No more scarred knees from shinnying up trees. From now on you're expected to look pretty and conduct yourself to match. For a first (or twenty-first), pink is good, but it's not the only possibility. . . . Whatever colors you choose (all lipsticks are basically variations of red), the effect must be clean and perfect.[5]

This made your first lipstick not just a milestone, but a sort of glam bat mitzvah or communion in which you accepted your adult responsibilities for your looks, and as "a Girl," looks were practically a part of your citizenship.

As to when you were handed that license, the editors were a little fuzzier. A subsequent issue contained a rather concerned letter to the editor: "Some of the 'firsts' in your January issue were a bit young. Most girls have their first lipstick and their first dressy shoes before they're seventeen!—A. M., Upper Darby, PA." To which *Seventeen* replied, "We think of *Seventeen* as a magazine for all high school girls, and we don't want to neglect either freshmen or seniors. Then, too, the age for first lipsticks and for dress-up clothes varies from group to group."[6] In other words, when to wear lipstick was a question you might ask your mother or your peer group.

In turn, mothers might turn to ladies' magazines to help them decide what was proper for their daughters. At some point, getting young women ready for makeup had been added to the infinite list of tasks that mothers were expected to be able to tackle with ease. One consistent piece of advice was to start preparing them young—really young. *Parents'* magazine assured mothers that starting beauty training with age-appropriate soap and cologne would pay off later, telling them that "Your encouragement and interest in her beauty care will please her and as a result she may even consult you and value your opinion when it's time when she's old enough to have her first lipstick! By the time she is thirteen and entering junior high, her friends are apt to be doing some highly secret experimenting with makeup. This is the time her trust in your judgement will be of great value. . . . Show her how a very pale pink lipstick is the most flattering shade anyone can wear, even on someone twice her age."[7]

Good Housekeeping took it a step further by suggesting that playing with makeup was important enough to involve the whole family. "When you have supplied your pretty, inquisitive, adventurous little daughter with her own toiletries and shown her how to use them, she would probably enjoy using them at her own little dressing table. (Dad might want to build a simple one out of plywood.) She will have a good basis for establishing good grooming habits and, what is more, will enjoy the process."[8] The article shared its page with an advertisement featuring the image of a blonde toddler making up in a mirror and captioned "My lip stick is 'Chap Stick.'"[9]

The care and development of the nuclear family was a central concern of the atomic age. Whether it was expressly stated or not, one of the goals at large was to raise a generation of Americans who understood the benefits and joys of gender roles, family togetherness, and purchasing power as a bulwark against the creeping threat of communism. Kicking off in earnest with the Red Scare of the World War I era through the 1959 Kitchen Debates between Soviet First Secretary Nikita Khrushchev and Vice President Richard Nixon in Moscow and continuing today, Americans continually have been besieged with the message that their way of life was superior but fragile. Reds, pinkos, commies, Bolsheviks, Marxists, collectivists, and socialists were everywhere and if we were not eternally vigilant against them, they would infiltrate the cracks of our society like Maoist termites, where they would eat away at the very foundations of life, liberty, and the pursuit of happiness until we were left with nothing but grim gray uniforms, rough toilet paper, and boring state-run TV.

For their part, women's magazines upheld this narrative by running any number of articles that gave readers an inside peek at life behind the iron curtain and the difficulties of keeping up even the most basic beauty routine in the face of Soviet shortages and Stalinist ideology. In an article titled "I Went to Moscow," chess champion Gisela Kahn Gresser notes her translator's absence of lipstick: "Her vivid blue eyes with their long lashes, heavily mascaraed (she used no other cosmetics) stood out in her pale, round face with a startling effect. When we became acquainted, I asked her one day why she made up only her eyes. 'Oh,' she said, 'if I should paint my face as you westerners do, I should look to vulgar.'" The author was also quick to point out the lack of merchandise in the Muscovite department stores and sniffs, "I assured her our stores are full."[10] For anyone pointing out the shortcomings of capitalism, it was a none-too-subtle reminder that at least we had limitless shades and finishes of red, pink, and coral and the freedom to buy and wear them.*

In "They Let Us Talk to the Russians," the editors of *Ladies' Home Journal* pressed exchange student Gay Humphrey for her impressions about her recent travels to the Soviet Union.

Q: Do Russian women use lipstick? Do they have cosmetics?

Gay: The more smartly dressed women wore lipstick as a general rule. But (our guide), Natasha scorned lipstick: "I don't need to paint my face and lips to make me look healthy." And she did have a perfectly lovely complexion. However, she was very interested in watching (my classmate) Jeri and me apply lipstick and mascara. And the maids—I would come back to my hotel room and find that my lipsticks had been screwed up to the top, and then the cover put back on, and they were always squashed.[11]

It's not mentioned but possible that housekeepers (or others) were checking the lipsticks for recording devices or other contraband items hidden in the cases. Given the ease of hiding items in the tube, the KGB would later develop an easily concealed single-shot 4.5mm pistol in the shape of a lipstick case nicknamed "The Kiss of Death" by Western collectors. Or it could've been a completely innocent gesture by people unfamiliar with our patented cases; it's hard to know. Either way, Gay also mentions the Russians were curious about nylon underwear, unemployment in the States, and if there were "naked women in all our ads."[12]

There were a few women in bathing suits and bath towels here and there in our advertising, but, generally speaking, nothing as lurid as the Russians suspected. The advertising industry itself was also experiencing a growth spurt as the advent of television gave messages a whole new medium to explore. One of the earliest adaptors was, of course, lipstick, as a couple visionary manufacturers realized the powerful potential of being in millions of American living rooms.

---

* Lipstick was difficult but not impossible to get in the postwar Soviet Union and the quality was very poor. There were other cosmetics including powder, cake mascara, perfumes, and lip pomades. One popular salve was Hopka, a form of petroleum jelly, which protected lips against Russian winters and was infused with mink fat.

Kiss proof. As inventor of kiss-proof lipstick and the first lipstick brand to realize the sales potential of TV, Hazel Bishop was an innovator who was ahead of her time. Her issues as a woman in the man's world of business remain emblematic. *Library of Congress*

Chief among them was Hazel Bishop and her "Kiss-Proof Lipstick." Born in Hoboken, New Jersey, in 1906 to a homemaker and prosperous businessman, Hazel Bishop seemed to be both bound for greatness and thwarted by her time. From the outset of her career, it seemed that time was literally not on her side; just as she was graduating from New York's Barnard College with a degree in chemistry and ambitions of attending med school, America was plunged into the Depression. Instead of getting her MD, she took night classes in chemistry at Columbia and found work as an organic chemist for Standard Oil, a vacuum company, and for the dermatologist who would go on to found Almay.

Naturally ambitious and encouraged by her mother, she experimented on her own time trying to develop a product that might find an audience and launch her as an independent businesswoman, including a pimple cream and facial tissues infused with menthol, neither of which came to fruition. In 1948, a chance encounter introduced her to the concept of "kiss-proof" lipstick in the form of an early French version of the product. Intrigued by the possibilities but not the formula itself (which she thought looked like dried blood), she began to experiment, literally whipping up her own version in her kitchen sink. Drawing on her background in chemistry, she hit upon the notion of adding bromo acids, which gave her formula the lasting power she was looking for. According to one article, "It took 300 'cookings' to find the right formula, she said. But how kiss-proof is the lipstick actually? Ask this of Miss Bishop and she will grin and state in her best scientific voice; 'It depends on the amount of friction involved.'"[13]

The resulting "Hazel Bishop's No-Smear Lipstick" officially launched in 1950 at Lord & Taylor's Fifth Avenue flagship store at $1 per tube. By the time the store closed that day, her entire run of the product was sold out. Hazel had cooked up something the market really wanted. As 1951 rolled around, she was the first woman to grace the cover of *Business Week*, accompanied by the headline "Woman Chemist Hits Jackpot."[14] Although Hazel had a hit, what she didn't have was capital to expand her business. Enter her business partner (and future nemesis), Raymond Specter. The legendary ad man knew an opportunity when he saw it, having already built a career by turning the Lone Ranger into a national phenomenon using the power of radio advertising.

In exchange for a large share of stock in the company, Specter would add mass media power to Bishop's chemistry and marketing savvy, thereby launching the six original shades into a multimillion-dollar empire using the nascent—but growing—reach of television. An early adopter, Specter took the ad dollars that had previously gone to radio and plowed them into TV airtime, sponsoring shows like *This Is Your Life* and *The Martha Raye Show*. Television wasn't just new in some corners, it was suspect and considered lowbrow by the higher-end brands, like Arden and Rubinstein, who refused to use it as an advertising channel for a number of years. But Specter saw something in those little black-and-white screens. Through them the audience at home could see the product's promise (if not its colors) for themselves via a side-by-side comparison that would surely translate into sales. For Hazel Bishop, this demo consisted of asking a show's hostess to draw an X on her palm with both Hazel Bishop and a competitor's lipstick and give it a good rub with a tissue. This left the other company's product smeared everywhere while the smear-proof held fast. Within four years, the lipstick that claimed it "stays on until you take it off" accounted for 25 percent of the overall market and about $10 million in sales.

All of which should have cemented Hazel's reputation as a business whiz, leaving her bulletproof in the industry she was dominating. Instead, voicing her opinions about how the business should operate marked her as a pushy broad and set her up for a fight with Specter and her all-male board. What followed were lawsuits and countersuits, wherein it was revealed she controlled "slightly less than 8 percent of the stock"[15] in the company that bore her name. Financially outgunned and literally outmanned in her proxy fight, by 1954 she could see what was coming and chose to take a buyout rather than fight herself into bankruptcy. Hazel Bishop Inc. limped on without Hazel Bishop, but Specter was (by several high-profile media accounts) a notoriously difficult jerk when it came to negotiations and, as a result, ended up losing his golden-goose programming slot on *The $64,000 Question* game show to Revlon when his demands on the network became too much and too public.[16] Not long after, he lost his seat in the boardroom entirely when the company was acquired by an equity firm[17] in 1959, which then turned over the reins to a "former Shanghai café bouncer"[18] in 1960 and merged the whole thing with a lanolin producer in 1961.[19] The brand hung on for a while but never recovered enough to be a major player again.

A handful of women had launched beauty companies successfully before the 1950s and certainly would again, but the trajectory of Hazel's company feels somehow emblematic of the era itself. During the Depression and World War II, women had entered the workforce in huge numbers out of necessity, agency, and patriotism. Because of the sheer number of women workers, things had shifted for a time. Who knows how many might have pursued careers of all kinds if they had not been forced out to create jobs for returning soldiers. A great number of women had seen what was possible beyond homemaking and might have continued in that way if the cultural climate didn't constantly remind them that their worth was as wives and mothers. Female executives were a novelty and a largely unwelcome one. As for Hazel herself, she may have been ahead of her time as a corporate officer, but she also may have had the last laugh in terms of long-term success. A popular speaker at industry conferences, she would invent some more household helpers, spend years as a successful stockbroker specializing in the beauty industry, and eventually would become a professor at New York's Fashion Institute of Technology, where she held the Revlon Chair in Cosmetics Marketing.

Fig 7.2 The new look. Trans pioneer Christine Jorgensen adjusts her lipstick in the ladies' room of the Stork Club. Her postoperative appearance would challenge many Americans' long-held notions of gender. *Library of Congress*

The expectations of the era, professionally and personally, made being a woman in the public eye no easy feat, particularly if she was trailblazing in high heels. Christine Jorgensen, for example, faced intense scrutiny when she returned to her native New York in 1952 after her travels to Denmark, with dozens of reporters and photographers snapping pictures and shouting questions about her outfit, her makeup, her future career plans. Neither a pop sensation nor a movie star, Christine was something entirely new to most Americans. Named George William Jorgensen Jr. at birth and raised in the Bronx, she had served as an army file clerk during World War II and now emerged publicly into the spotlight as the country's first openly postoperative, male-to-female transgender citizen. At a time when even living room easy chairs came gendered in matching his-and-her models, it was a great deal to absorb.

To give their readers a sense of Christine's transformation, one news syndicate sent out a pair of male and female reporters to get their expert takes. Their accounts were, as you can imagine, disparate:

- "She's No Jane Russell, Says Male Reporter": If you shut your eyes when she spoke, you'd think a man was talking. But her gestures with a cigarette were gracefully feminine. Her legs, what could be seen of them, were smooth and trim. However, the planes of her face were flat and hard. She wore a lot of makeup that gave her skin a pinkish tint.[20]

- "To a Woman, Chris Belongs to the Tribe": Christine is not only a female, she's a darn good-looking female. . . . Christine wore an expert job of makeup: thick pancake, bright true red lipstick that set off very good teeth when she smiled and dark mascara and eyebrow pencil to accent her greenish-blue eyes.[21]

In the absence of any existing public discourse about the construct of gender and the complicated nature of biological sex, interest turned to the banal trappings of Christine's feminine presentation, namely her lipstick habits and the shapeliness of her ankles. On this latter point, at least, everyone seemed to agree that they were very attractive.

The young woman who had come down the stairs at Idlewild Airport "clutching a makeup kit in one hand and a lipstick-stained cigarette in the other"[22] held the public imagination and the media spotlight for quite a while as both something of a celebrity and a freak. Unsure of what to make of someone who had so willingly crossed the gender line and embraced the outward trappings of femininity, she managed a successful career as a cabaret singer who attracted audiences as much for a chance to see her up close as for her charms onstage. Self-aware and comfortable in her choices, she entertained audiences with her rendition of "I Enjoy Being a Girl," sold her life story to the press, wrote a memoir, lectured as an LGBTQ pioneer, and was eventually the subject of a movie about her life story. (That is, not counting Ed Wood's trash masterpiece *Glen or Glenda*, which was partially inspired by Christine's transformation, along with Wood's own fetish for women's wear.) She paved the way for generations of gender nonconforming people in the years to come but probably didn't move the needle too much at the beginning. Lipstick, powder, and "trim ankles"[23] will remain largely a female pursuit (with some risk-taking exceptions) for years to come.

In the meantime, the consumerism of the 1950s would remain highly gendered. So much so that Detroit would offer a car specifically designed for what male engineers assumed the ladies looked for in an automobile. The Dodge La Femme wasn't strictly a new model, and it was not ergonomically designed for bodies that were shorter or smaller, nor did it offer an easy-to-use trunk or child-friendly seats. Instead, it was a paint job (pink, naturally) and a package of options available on the stock Royal Lancer for an extra $134. The two-door coupe (not exactly ideal for carpooling) came with a matching purse, raincoat, umbrella, compact, cigarette case, and, of course, a lipstick. It wasn't well advertised and never quite caught on with whichever women it was meant for and was discontinued just two model years after it launched. Lesson learned, Chrysler's girly La Comtesse model stalled at the concept car stage, and generations of married women would continue to be offered the same old station wagons and minivans without nifty accessories or two-tone finishes in "orchid."

The prosperity of the era also meant that more people could imagine themselves enjoying the comforts of the middle class, including Americans of color. In particular, a dedicated set of publications allowed Black Americans to see themselves as proud, successful tastemakers in much the same way that white families always had. Although not specifically about fashion or beauty, magazines such as *Jet* and *Ebony* featured glamorous starlets, singers, and fashion designers of color alongside other prosperous professionals in law, medicine, and education, in between a healthy dose of advertising for shiny new cars, top-shelf liquors, electric organs, chrome-plated appliances, and other trappings of the suburban good life. Their advertising also offered opportunity in the form of ads for Lucky Heart Cosmetics' representatives. Lucky Heart was founded by two Jewish chemists in 1923 out of Memphis, Tennessee. Morris Shapiro and Joseph Menke knew when they saw an opportunity in an underserved market. They built their business on the same door-to-door sales model that would later make Avon a household name. Unlike Avon, and because their offerings included gender neutral items like hairdressing pomades, Lucky Heart encouraged male representatives. "My wife was making so much money as a Lucky Heart representative, I started taking orders too. I made $30 to $40 in spare hours," claimed James Campbell of Texas in one of the company's ads.[24] Whether that was true for most reps is hard to say, but the proposition of self-employment and extra money was certainly tempting.

Interestingly, Lucky Heart didn't expressly state that its products were designed for the Black or Latinx community, but instead subtly offered a line of "Color Keyed Cosmetics," which translated to colors suited to a darker range of skin tones that couldn't otherwise be found on store shelves (and certainly not in department stores). Additionally, for many African American consumers, the direct sales method was an ideal way to purchase. During the years when Brown vs. Board of Education was still being fought in the court of public opinion, many white-owned businesses didn't welcome their business, let alone cater to their needs. According to its copy, Lucky Heart wasn't just pushing the newest shades, it was empowering the people by offering representatives a "Glamorous, Dignified Way to a Better Living."[25] Which was a potent message on the pages of magazines that had featured everyone from the effervescent Dorothy Dandridge to the mutilated Emmett Till on their covers.

That dichotomy of glamour and cruelty somehow encapsulates America in the 1950s, which was both a rose-colored boom time and a stress test of our ability to accept how fast the world was changing around us. Heading into the 1960s, this rift between the prosperous surface of an economic boom and the social disparity roiling below would grow even more pointed until it actually became a part of the civil rights movement and the ensuing conversation about who and what was beautiful. The mass media conversation regarding something as commonplace as lipstick would make it even clearer than ever who was clinging to the past (that probably never really existed) and who was trying to shape the future. Further, youth and young people would become even more central to that discussion as manufacturers and advertisers tried to stay "with it" and sell lipstick to a generation that was rejecting the rules that it had spent years learning.

CHAPTER EIGHT

THE COSMETIC COUNTERCULTURE
The 1960s

Shades of the Decade
Revlon Swinging Pink
Estée Lauder Frosted Peach
Yardley of London Chelsea Pink
Max Factor's Pink-a-Pale
Avon White Icing

Even by first lady standards, Jackie Kennedy was almost unnaturally cool and well put together, so much so that even contemporary fashion critics wondered how she did it. "Does (she) wear Hazel Bishop's new no-smear lipstick or are her gloves made from some special no-stain fabric? It has been noticed that the First Lady has a few gestures that most women would turn pale before using if they were wearing immaculate white gloves."[1] More likely, years of training in the social graces had taught her never to touch her mouth or fidget or do anything else that might soil a pair of pristine gloves, but the true details of her sleight of hand remain unexplained. That said, it's been reported that she was a lifelong adherent of Elizabeth Arden's refined pinks and reds. Symbolically it seems that the 1960s swept in with the cool elegance of Camelot and Jackie's modish dresses, chic bouffant hair, and fresh pink lip, and, somehow, snuck out with Pat Nixon's out-of-sync style, dowdy, polyester dresses, fusty bouffant hair, and dull pink lipstick. A lot can happen in a decade. Particularly one as tumultuous and norm-smashing as the 1960s, in which advertisers would have to learn to sell to a generation that was both incredibly savvy and rejected material trappings in favor of free love, dropping out, and flower power. White-glove formality would be out, doing your own thing would be in.

The decade is also marked by a new obsession with youth. Not new exactly, since appearing youthful and therefore desirable has always been one of the stated goals of skin care and fashion, but with young people specifically. If the advertising wizards of the 1950s found that teenagers had money to spend, the admen of the 1960s absolutely counted on them as central to everything from creating lifestyle fads to driving the political conversation. In 1960, *Ladies' Home Journal* underlined the power they would have in numbers: "A new generation is coming up. Seventeen million young people in the country, age 13 to 18 years old, are almost a nation within a nation; they are more like each other in their tastes, the pastimes, their passions, the way they look, the way they act than ever before."[2] For the beauty industry and its media, this interest in their likes and dislikes went beyond the best way to parent, this was a professional curiosity; there was power in that junior nation.

The *New York Times* stated that "The teenager, whose formidable purchasing power was once all but ignored by advertisers; has become the most pampered of purchasers. Advertisers lavish their attention—and their advertising dollars—on the meticulous study of teenage habits and foibles to uncover emerging trends."[3] The article particularly notes the coveted market of young women who looked to *Seventeen* for beauty guidance. "The typical teenage girl has acquired an aura of sophistication in recent years, and *Seventeen* has adapted itself to this change. The once girlish, almost giggly, format has been brought up to date and today's *Seventeen* is awash in bouffant hairstyles and smart-looking attire."[4] Its advertisers naturally fell in line with the changes, adapting their messaging to keep up with the times but always in an innocent, all-American, girl-next-door way. The *Times* also noted that there was an age limit to the nature of advertising, since that magazine didn't take ads for liquor, cigarettes, hair dye, or wedding dresses.

The urge to marry young was still widespread when what we think of as the "Swinging Sixties" kicked off; according to Gallup's polling, the sexual revolution hadn't quite gathered the necessary munitions yet.

Namely "the pill," which would debut in 1960 and become legal for single and married women in all states after the 1965 Supreme Court ruling of Griswold v. Connecticut declared contraception a matter of personal privacy. Until that happened, things would remain relatively old-timey, with "almost all of our young women [in the Gallup study] between 16 and 21 expect to be married by 22."[5] Moreover, they really wanted to buy stuff, namely homes, clothes, and makeup—a lot of makeup. So much makeup. "Dr. Gallup's trained and seasoned researchers expressed considerable surprise at how beauty-conscious this young American girl is. She devours beauty news and tips—and overwhelmingly (88 percent) relies on magazines for them. . . . Lipstick is standard equipment; after putting lipstick on, the girls beg to differ."[6] So it was generally agreed that everyone had to have a lipstick, but not everyone needed an eyeliner—or a husband for that matter. Attitudes around sex, dating, and marriage would change soon enough, but entire industries were betting on lipstick continuing to be an ingredient in all of those things.

Charles Revson was willing to wager heavily on lipstick futures and was handsomely rewarded. He already had built an entire empire by figuring out what women wanted. Although in a 1960 *Cosmo* profile titled "What I Don't Know about Women" he demurred a bit, insisting "Plenty." He then, however, launched into a rubric about how not knowing was a sort of knowledge of its own.

> But what you don't know about women is the key to understanding them. *Never*, with women take *anything* for granted—every woman always has some unknown quantity. She is always changing—that is her never-ending desire. She is always creating new mysteries about herself; her clothes and fashions change, she changes her makeup, she changes mentally and emotionally. By aiming for real beauty potential, she can affect herself spiritually.[7]

Whether he actually believed that philosophy or it just sounded right for an article that was designed to soften his public image is immaterial. By the time he was explaining women to the female readership of *Cosmopolitan*, he had grown Revlon from a small nail polish outfit founded in the depths of the Depression (the *l* was added by an early business partner, Charles Lachman) to a multinational conglomerate doing billions of dollars in business in everything from cosmetics to perfume to hair care under multiple brand names. A stickler for color and detail, he was typical of corporate titans of his era as both a terror to his staff and a genius with marketing.

The son of Jewish immigrants, Revson was raised in New Hampshire and seemed driven to succeed from the beginning. He had no specific interest in cosmetics initially, founding Revlon seemingly out of spite when a nail polish company he had been working for refused to promote him. However, once he'd set his aim, he was relentless to the point of obsession. According to one biographer, when the company was getting off the ground, he was a travelling salesman for the brand. Upon checking into his room in any given hotel, Revson would quality-check the product himself by putting on lipstick before bed and ordering an early wake-up call to see how it was wearing. In later years, this perfectionism would take the form of scorching tirades against his long-suffering advertising staff, which would continue until all ads met his exacting standards. Albeit a nightmare for the ad department, he was a boon for accounts receivable, as his sense for what would catch on worked most of the time. His Fire and Ice campaign, for example, set a new standard in beauty advertising by daring to presume that women bought lipsticks for their own pleasure and self-expression rather than simply to attract men. Debuting in 1952, it featured legendary model Dorian Leigh and came with a racy fifteen-point questionnaire that encouraged women to envision themselves as "a *new* American beauty." Answer "yes" to eight or more questions like "Have you ever danced with your shoes off?" "When a recipe calls for *one* dash of bitters, do you think it's better with *two*?" "Have you ever wanted to wear an ankle bracelet?" and you could consider yourself "made for 'Fire and Ice.'" This test was less about catching Mr. Right or fitting in with the "in crowd" and more about considering your own personal tastes. It was a preview of things to come.

The new decade would build on that success. Throughout the era, Revlon lipstick ads act as a case study in adapting to the shifts of fashion and values by nimbly navigating their way through every look from high midcentury glamour to earthy hippie chic. In 1960 they were still selling their tried-and-true mix of sex appeal and glam;* Berry Bon Bon was

---

* The ad hearkens back to the Fire and Ice success in more than one way; the sequin evening gown is very similar and the model, who bears an uncanny resemblance to Dorian Leigh, is actually her sister and fellow supermodel, Suzy Parker.

touted as "A strong-sweet red. . . . You won't gain anything but admirers."[8] By 1962, they had moved on to a more mod look with "Colors Avant Garde," a set of pale pinks with winking names like Blasé Apricot and Swinging Pink as a "New low-key look for today's new breed of beauty . . . bored with yesterday's fashion cliches, restless for tomorrow's look today."[9] In 1967, they were challenging women to rethink how hip they were with copy that challenged them to embrace a glossier look in the "The with-it wet mouth,"[10] and "Pale-power!"[11] The latter is a really odd bit of messaging in the wake of the civil rights movement and the Black Panthers' call for "All power to the people," but one that attempted to capture the moment. When 1969 rolled around, the company seemed to be searching for a way to appeal to those flower children who'd decided to go wild and free by "Un-nouncing Un-lipstick by Natural Wonder."[12]

In 1968, Cosmopolitan attempted to sum up "The Compleat (Hippie) Girl," using a girl named Candy who had gone from her parents' middle-class home to living on the streets of San Francisco's Haight-Ashbury district, "She never irons her clothes. She wears no makeup or stockings, and she needs no money for fares, or newspapers, or dry cleaning."[13] In other words, she was pretty much an advertiser's nightmare. After spending decades trying to refine their messaging, marketers and manufacturers were confronted with the new reality of a generation that wasn't buying what they were selling. At ground level, a lot had changed since that 1960 Gallup poll. It was as if, in the fallout from the civil rights movement, the Vietnam War protests, and a second wave of feminism, an entire generation had reexamined the American Dream of consumerism and conformity and found it wanting.

Popular texts, like Betty Friedan's best-selling *The Feminine Mystique*, were quick to point out that even women who achieved the goals that years of mass media had set out for them—namely wife and mother—had discovered that such roles weren't as fulfilling as promised and that they might want a little more out of life. Feminism, at least in some segments of the movement, was ready to chuck out the proverbial baby with the bathwater and redefine the expectations of what it was to be a woman in this society. Was makeup compatible with feminism or was it just another scam designed to make women feel insecure and reinforce gender norms? For many activists, the answer was the latter: beauty was part and parcel of the male gaze and just another form of oppression, and it was time to throw off its yoke and take a stand for equality. These were fair questions, and it was past time to start asking them. For years, the ideal had been relentless in its requirements, uniform in its worship of thin, white, girlish women as the ideal, and ever shifting in its demands to keep up with the latest style craze—gamine or voluptuous, sexy or innocent, wife or whore.

What would happen if women just stopped buying into it all—both literally and conceptually—and set their own course? A number of feminists were game to find out. In 1968, a group of them picketed the most ossified and symbolic of events: the Miss America Pageant. Tired of watching dozens of quiet, congenial women paraded in front of judges and audiences like so many terriers at the Westminster Kennel Club, a number of activists decided to launch a protest that would send up the "ludicrous standards that have enslaved the American woman."† To underline their point, they filled a garbage can with bras, girdles, curlers, lipsticks, high heels, and other everyday trappings of womanhood; what they did *not* do was set fire to it. Police wouldn't permit it for alleged safety reasons, but just the same, that's the way it's misremembered, and bra burning (and not the disposal of lipsticks or girdles) has somehow become associated with the aims and methods of feminism.

Columnist Art Buchwald grumbled from his nationally syndicated column, "If the average American woman gave up all her makeup products, she would look like [singer] Tiny Tim, and there would be no reason at all for the American male to have anything to do with her." He was being somewhat facetious but also not.

> The protesters think they're bringing about a revolution by discarding all feminine makeup, but actually they're turning back the clock to pre-civilization days when men and women did look and smell alike. . . . If the women in Atlantic City wanted to picket the Miss America Beauty Pageant because it is lily white, that is one thing, and if they wanted to picket because it is a bore, that is also a legitimate excuse. But when they start asking young American women to burn their brassieres and throw away their false eyelashes, then we say dissent in this country has gone too far.[14]

---

† The winning contestant, Miss Debra Dene Barnes of Kansas, didn't agree and happened to play the theme from *Born Free* on the piano as her talent portion.

Lipstick in public. Formerly a well-kept, boudoir secret of Victorian beauty routines, improvements in packaging, the advent of motion pictures, and a more mobile population all led to lipstick's adoption as an everyday, on-the-go essential for the modern flapper. *Library of Congress*

Red means go. The Depression marked an unprecedented number of women working outside the home, and despite economic uncertainty, lipstick remained a must-have item for most women. The result is advertising that speaks to both women's busy lives and the implied need for beauty. *Library of Congress*

Beauty is your duty. World War II created new roles for women and made lipstick a part of the war effort. With women of every race and class filling "men's jobs" for the first time, lipstick became a patriotic duty, a form of propaganda, and a normalizing force. *Library of Congress*

The beauty boom. The prosperity of the postwar 1950s reflected an economic boom time and a push for all-out glamour. Lipstick was now the norm in a society returning to the nuclear family model of domesticity and a bulwark against the threats (real and perceived) of communism. *Duke University*

Lucky Heart "Color-Keyed" Cosmetics
can bring you $65 to $250 extra, regularly!

Easy Earning Plan turns Spare Hours into Cash Money

A few pleasant calls a day turn spare hours into $65 to $250 regular income. Folks welcome you because you bring the newest and latest in fine cosmetics to their homes.

If you want to turn your own dreams into reality, money can do it. There is no limit to how much you can make with Lucky Heart Cosmetics.

Yes, good things happen to you when you start with Lucky Heart. You get that good feeling of having lots of extra money—of being able to buy the things you want—of really living. Anyone, any age, anywhere can show and demonstrate Lucky Heart Cosmetics. We show you how to start earning money right away, simply, easily, step-by-step. Everything you need to get started is furnished.

As a Lucky Heart Cosmetics Representative you merely call on people you already know and like—in your neighborhood, at work, church and club.

Show them Lucky Heart's new, exclusive "Color-Keyed" Make-Up Chart. Let them try Lucky Heart's "Color-Keyed" cosmetics, perfumes and hair products. Let them see and decide for themselves how much better and more flattering Lucky Heart Cosmetics are. That's why they'll want Lucky Heart Cosmetics and when you'll start making money. For more money and a better way of life for yourself and your family fill in coupon and mail it today.

FREE $10 DISPLAY KIT OFFER!

Just mail coupon now for your Lucky Heart Cosmetic Display Kit. It's worth $10. Showing the kit can bring you $65 to $250 or more regularly. It contains 6 full size, fast selling Lucky Heart products for demonstration, plus samples and Perfume Demonstrators. The kit is yours FREE when you become a Lucky Heart Cosmetics Representative. Fill in and mail coupon with $1 to help cover postage and handling. Do it now! You'll be richer for it!

©1959 Lucky Heart Cosmetics, Memphis, Tenn.

Lucky Heart COSMETICS

400 MULBERRY STREET, Dept. 18, Memphis 2, TENNESSEE

Lucky Heart Cosmetics, Dept. 18, Memphis 2, Tenn.

Please send my $10 Cosmetic Display Kit prepaid. I enclose $1 to help cover postage and handling. If I am not completely satisfied you will refund my $1.

Name_____

Address_____

City_____Zone____State____

☐ Please send me more information

Color-keyed cosmetics. Women of color have long been underrepresented in the industry as both consumers and entrepreneurs, save for a few companies that recognized their beauty and buying power. Lucky Heart Cosmetics, for example, was one of the few companies that catered to different skin tones and buying needs. *Courtesy of Lucky Heart Cosmetics*

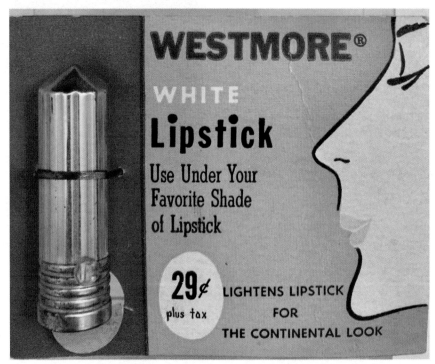

It's a mod world. The 1960s were an adjustment for the beauty industry as it struggled to meet the moment of a youth culture that was rejecting long-established norms and makeup in general. Companies like Westmore of Hollywood tried to adapt with offerings that recognized new fads and changing tastes. *Courtesy of the House of Westmore*

Pretty in punk. In the wake of feminism, the 1960s counterculture, civil rights, and other massive societal shifts, the "me generation" increasingly viewed makeup choices as self-expression rather than simply beauty or conformity. Musician Patricia Morrison, pictured here, pioneered the dark beauty of goth for one such subculture. *Alice Bag, Wikimedia Commons*

Hello Dolly. More than just a pretty face, Dolly Parton is one of a number of entertainers and entrepreneurs who has both used and subverted the classic trappings of femininity to build their own empires. For some, her hyperfeminine image belies her skills as a businesswoman, songwriter, and philanthropist. *Wikimedia Commons*

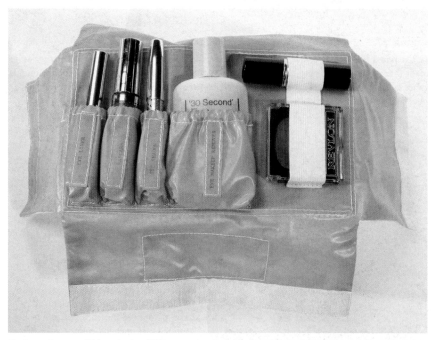

Going places. Although the 1980s saw women continue to make strides in a large number of professional fields, the pressure to maintain a polished appearance remained—and even accelerated—in some industries. NASA even engineered this makeup kit for the first American woman in space, Sally Ride, on the assumption that she would want to put on a full face of makeup for her historic shuttle flight. She did not. *Smithsonian Institution*

Drag queen meets riot grrrl. The 1990s marked a mainstreaming of subculture with performers like RuPaul and Courtney Love emerging as icons and creating a long-term impact on lipstick trends and the way coming generations would view gender and feminism. *Getty Images*

The birth of the influencer. At the dawn of the internet age, a new generation of makeup artists were learning how to monetize their expertise and proximity to fame, a model that would lay the foundations for the rise of the influencer. Kevyn Aucoin, in particular, was adept at creating trends and leveraging his own celebrity. *Courtesy of the Makeup Museum*

The red scare. Alexandria Ocasio-Cortez's role as a beauty influencer (as well as a politician) marks both a new era of inclusion in beauty and a revival of early-twentieth-century fears of socialist infiltration. *Wikimedia Commons*

As it had been in World War II—and really since the dawn of gender norms—beauty was still your duty. According to the smaller counter-protest launched by those who worried that tossing makeup would have a grave impact on "America the Beautiful," the concept of a generation of women without makeup was frightening. Former runner-up and Miss Green Bay Terry Meewsen showed up with a hand-painted sign that read "There's Only One Thing Wrong with Miss America. She's Beautiful." The placard was pinned to her dress with a Nixon-for-president button.[15] Fictitious, binary battle lines were being drawn that would define the conversation in mass media for decades to come. Women had to make a choice: they could be beautiful or they could be feminists. For now, any-way, the message was that you couldn't have it all.

Outside of that sphere, however, not every pageant or fashion show was a negative. Crowned the same night as the apocryphal bra-burning protest, nineteen-year-old Saundra Williams was named Miss Black America in a separate Atlantic City pageant. ‡ Of her win, she told *Seventeen* magazine, "For years I'd been brainwashed into thinking that beauty consisted of straight hair, a thin, straight nose, and thin lips. The contest proved what I just recently learned—that Black is beautiful."[16] The phrase "Black is beautiful," which would come to define the struggle to stretch the borders of beauty ideals to include African American men and women, has origins in the work of photographer Kwame Brathwaite, particularly his 1962 show "Naturally '62: The Original African Coif-fure and Fashion Extravaganza Designed to Restore Our Racial Pride and Standards," which was among the first to feature all-Black models sporting their natural hair and African-inspired fashions. Reviewed by the *Pittsburgh Courier*, the reporter marveled at the boldness of untreated African American hair, saying, "Fads come and go but two things that are still swinging in this Telstar age are the twist and natural hairdos. . . . Tied up in this trend is a protest against injustice and recognition of African culture. . . . Some lovely women in New York wear the natural hairdo and they look very sexy and ferine (that's wild, man)."[17] Buried in the slang and attempts to be hip is the dawning recognition that Black women might

---

‡ The first Black contestant, Cheryl Adrienne Browne Hollingsworth, competed the next year. She earned the title of Miss Iowa of 1970 and was admitted to compete in the pag-eant when the rules committee finally removed the 1930s-era rule that "contestants must be of good health and of the white race."

have their own sense of style separate from the blonde-haired, blue-eyed model that had long dominated advertising imagery.

Relatedly, the cosmetics industry also started to notice that Black women also were consumers of beauty and might like quality products that actually spoke to them. In 1965, Flori Roberts launched the first department store brand under her own name that was designed specifically for women of color. As a marketing consultant, she had heard Black models complain about the lack of available foundation shades and set out to launch a high-end company that met that demand. Her ability to sell the Flori Roberts concept and acquire some prime floor space in posh department stores may have something to do with the fact that she herself was white. Regardless, it was a step toward inclusion and Black consumers rejoiced. The Black-owned *Amsterdam News* welcomed the change. "It was not too long ago that blood red, purple, and grape lipsticks and nut brown powders were all a black woman could purchase at the five and dime. . . . Well those days are gone—and apparently gone forever—since the beauty of the black woman has become a reality for all the world to see, know, appreciate, and, yes, love."[18]

The mainstream, largely white press was a little more awkward in its understanding.

> Black is beautiful, the cosmetic industry agrees, but why not make it more so? The question was posed at a conference on cosmetics for negroes. Cosmetics for the $35-million negro market is the industry's newest challenge says Steven Tuckman, publisher of *Cosmetics Fair* magazine. "Negro women are no longer following the white image," Tuckman said. Instead they are vibrant with the awareness that they are Black and beautiful.[19]

While Black women (and companies that served them) were realizing their worth, the press was still pretty slow on the uptake. There were only a handful of successful African American models appearing on the pages of *Vogue*, *Cosmopolitan*, and other fashion magazines, and a scant few in national ads. Editorial copy that spoke to them would be scarce for years (and would fall into problematic cliché and presumption for a while afterward). However, for all its old-fashioned airs, *Ladies' Home Journal* would actually be the first publication to break the color barrier with Naomi Sims as its cover model in November 1968. The major fashion magazines would hold out until the 1970s. In some small way, however, the decade did mark an opening of doors that previously had been for "whites only."

The question remained, how to reconcile all women's changing standards and the manufacturers' need to keep moving product? Simply put, if you can't beat 'em, join 'em. Advertising and editorial text would be refocused to be younger, hipper, and sympathetic to movements—whatever they might be. A little mercenary, a little sincere—since much of the writing staff were themselves young and conscious of what was going on—it was a change that would shift a chunk of American marketing to the sort of "values marketing" that could make Pepsi "the choice of a new generation" (1963) and Coke an international symbol of peace (i.e., "I'd Like to Buy the World a Coke," 1971), rather than simply fizzy sugar water. If soda could transform itself into a movement, lipstick could, too.

In addition to the mod fabulous and boho chic imagery being used in ads, the editorial language was jumping on the flower child trends in its own you-can-buy-this-look way. *Family Weekly* suggested a drug-free trip via mood lipsticks.

> To experiences psychedelic, now add a new one—wearing makeup that shines, sparkles, colors, and expands the senses. . . . Cover Girl offers a chemical happening with their new trio of frosted lipsticks called Crazy Sticks. A blue stick turns pink on your lips, a green becomes peachy, and a beige intensifies the natural. The lipsticks can also be worn under other shades to open up a whole new color spectrum.[20]

Sounds far out, but chemically it probably wasn't all that different from grandma's Tangee, which reacted to the natural pH on the wearers' lips. It was, however, an old favorite smartly repackaged for a generation that was turning on and tuning in with LSD, mushrooms, and other recreational hallucinogens—or at least dressing like they were.

Even the staid society pages of *Town & Country* were feeling the vibes of the moment in their own way by featuring debutantes in designer peasant dresses and encouraging readers to let their freak flag fly in the season's hot new styles.

> [The] key phrase for the sixties, as every swinger in good standing knows is "your own thing"—that is definitely the makeup trend for fall '68. . . . From Helena Rubinstein—Makeup that Turns You On! The Subliminal

Look! But definitely not for the faint of heart. You can easily get hooked on it—but, oh, how you'll love being hooked. . . . Subliminal lips are shot with gold—or reversible; one for day, one for night. Both ways you get a built-in lighting system.

Your choice of lipstick was now both a happening and a declaration of your own style. Personal grooming was getting even more personal for those who eventually morph into the me generation. Sure, there was still the must-have look of the moment that everyone was wearing, but more and more ads and articles were talking to you, what made you tick and what made you special. Lipstick would become another way you, the individual, could declare yourself to the world.

Looking forward, the industry had some ideas about what was next for it. After a number of years of the futurist rule breaking of mod fashion and the antiestablishment free-for-all of hippie chic, industry analysts envisioned the same sort of conservative backlash that was enveloping the politics of the Nixon era. Speaking to the powerful industry journal *Women's Wear Daily* in June 1968 just after the assassination of Bobby Kennedy, some power players were already looking forward to a more sedate forecast.

There is talk of a conservative backlash . . . and some fashion intellectuals think it is coming. Others disagree. They believe fashion to be something apart, that it will not be affected by the great events of the day. But violence in the country, riots in Europe, the long hard war . . . convince some fashion leaders the time is now for a new conservatism. . . .

Lawrence of Revlon: I have always had a conservative view of makeup.

Helen Van Slyke of Helena Rubinstein: I feel the Real Woman is coming back. I do think we are moving into an era where women want to look pretty, elegant, and non-kooky. I do think the age thing is a hang up with women anyway.

Robert Granitz of Charles of the Ritz: We have gone through several wars and women have never given up their lipstick. If anything, they will put on a brave face . . . if there was to be a reaction.[21]

Fashion was tired of interesting times; whether public appetites agreed with this backswing and consumers were ready for less revolutionary looks would remain to be seen.

Heading into the next decade, beauty had moved by leaps and bounds in terms of inclusivity and convention. Now that lipstick was the norm, women were being told they didn't need to conform, or that they could conform in their own way, or that nonconformance was actually the hot new trend. There were a lot of conflicting messages all at once, and even those with the biggest, most valuable platforms were learning how to keep up with a new set of values. How much further the messaging around lipstick could be pushed in terms of race, gender, age, and availability depended only on who was doing the pushing.

NEVER MIND THE LIPSTICKS
The 1970s

At the dawn of the disco era, some people were more than ready to sparkle. According to at least one account, during the early hours of June 28, 1969, Marsha P. Johnson sent a shot glass sailing through a barroom mirror inside the Stonewall Inn in New York City and declared, as it shattered, "I got my civil rights." More than a bar fight, this was a declaration of war on oppression, police brutality, and gender norms and a turning point in the gay pride movement. Tired of being harassed, beaten, and carted off to jail for the crime of being themselves, some of the bar's patrons reached their snapping point that night and launched several days of rioting that would shift a generation into action. By the same time the next year, Marsha was marching up Sixth Avenue in the city's first gay pride parade. She was determined to blaze a trail and she was going to wear a bright shade of lipstick at each step.

Pay it no mind. Marsha P. Johnson helped launch the gay pride movement and struggled to find her place within it as a trans woman of color. For her, lipstick was a means of self-expression and a civil right. *Courtesy of the Lesbian & Gay Services Center Archives*

She explained her involvement to the *Village Voice* newspaper a decade later, saying

We used to sit in our little 42nd Street hotel rooms—"hot spring hotels," they used to call them—and party and get high and think about walking down the street someday and not worry about getting busted by the police. That was a dream we all had, sitting in those hotel rooms or in the queens' tanks of the jails. So, honey, when it came that night, I was ready to tip a few cars for a dream. It was that year—1969—when I finally went out in the street in drag full-time. I just said, "I don't give a shit," and I've been in drag most of the time since.[1]

In the years before popular language evolved to understand the nuances of gender difference, she was referred to in the press throughout the years as a drag queen, transvestite, and trans activist. No matter the label, Marsha was both a trailblazer and a rabble-rouser in her own community. Born Malcolm Michaels in Elizabeth, New Jersey, in 1945, she ran away to the city as a teenager where she survived the dangerous worlds of sex work, homelessness, and mental illness to eventually rechristen herself as Marsha P. Johnson. The "P.," she said, was short for "pay it no mind," her favorite response to questions about her gender.

Black, gay, and gender nonconforming, her very existence was a dangerous statement. It must be noted that choosing to appear in public in makeup was risky and had little support, since drag itself or "dressing as the opposite sex" was still illegal in New York in those years and punishable with jail time. She was something of an outsider among outsiders, with both the *New York Times* and the gay press struggling with the words to categorize her presence and that of those like her in the movement. The *Times* in 1970 described her cadre in the first pride march:

> Now at a time when Black, Puerto Ricans, Indians and young people are all refusing to acquiesce in the social values that relegate them to the nether worlds, many homosexuals are standing up and saying, "I'm proud, too. I'm equal and demand my rights." Those subscribing to such aggressive tactics include all the groups who marched last weekend from the "Queens"—men who wore lipstick and dresses.[2]

The gay press was also asking itself difficult questions. "Many Gays who support the Gay Liberation Movement stop short at transvestism. They feel that transvestites of either sex are going too far. They point out how the mass media depicts all of us in terms of stereotypes that seem to fit only transvestites."[3] Even within a burgeoning civil rights movement, initially there was some real fear of crossing gender lines for both gay men and women. Which for some, more timid activists, meant that lipstick could and should appear only on female faces for the time being and for the good of the movement.

Marsha continued to "pay it no mind" and pushed forward, founding the short-lived S.T.A.R. (Street Transvestites Action Revolutionaries) with friend Sylvia Rivera to give queer teens a place to stay and something of a support network. Struggling against poverty, racism, and transphobia, she continued to drift in and out of homelessness, mental health crises, and run-ins with the police. Still, she tried to keep up appearances, explaining that she "makes up at department store sample counters (this morning it was Lord and Taylor, but the regular rotation included Bloomingdale's, Macy's, Saks Fifth Avenue, and B. Altman). 'It's hard work, being beautiful, when you don't have a place. I do my best though,' Marsha drawled."[4] Beauty was to her, and to other pioneers of the LGBTQ movement, a civil right that was worth fighting for. Tragically, she was murdered by an unknown assailant in 1992, but her legacy remains for generations of

Personality crisis. Protopunk band the New York Dolls appear on a Dutch TV show in full, gender-bending glam. Their legacy as musicians is intertwined with their drag-inspired image. *Wikimedia Commons*

trans and nonbinary people and New York has commissioned a statue in her honor not far from where she fatefully tossed the "shot glass heard round the world."

Meanwhile across town, some men wearing makeup was only rock 'n' roll. The New York Dolls' 1973 debut album featured not just the band's name scrawled across the cover in pink lipstick, but all five members outfitted in unconvincing, but full, drag. Later inspiring such musically disparate sounds as Mötley Crüe and the Smiths, the Dolls would arrive on the scene ahead of their time, inspire both intense fandom and deep hatred, plant the seeds of everything from punk to hair metal, and sink into obscurity again—all of which reasonably can be attributed to their gender-bending, rock dandy style almost as much as their music. Although their tracks largely consisted of grungy, garage-rock versions of girl group–inspired pop tunes, they were lumped in with everyone from David Bowie's high-concept alien* to Alice Cooper's horror show, simply because of the makeup.

The *Boston Globe*'s rock critic Nathan Cobb sniped, "If we can be convinced that Alice Cooper, David Bowie, Lou Reed, and a few others all represent some sort of unified trend toward decadence, well, why not tack on the Dolls, too? These punks, word has it, were going to be kings (and queens) of what someone called 'ash can rock' and if you didn't like it someone might offer to break your elbows."[5] Cobb really did not like them or anyone else who had the temerity to add theatrical elements to their acts, and he was on a tear. Barely a week later, Cobb was pressing Lou Reed, who was then amid his own *Rock and Roll Animal* glam phase, about the Dolls and what he termed "fag rock, if you will." Reed promptly put him in his place, "A lot of our style today comes from transvestites. There is no such thing as 'fag rock,' or whatever you want to call it. There are simply people dealing with a subject heretofore taboo on the highly heterosexual rock stage and they are doing it in divergent styles."[6] For some people, it seemed like (straight) sex and drugs and rock 'n' roll was great, but men wearing lipstick and spandex was just perverse.

---

* Bowie's makeup looks at that time were perhaps a bit more acceptable, since they were less female impersonation and more stage persona. For his Aladdin Sane and Ziggy Stardust makeup, he collaborated with Elizabeth Arden–trained artist, Pierre LaRoche, who would also create Tim Curry's Dr. Frank N. Furter look for the *Rocky Horror Picture Show* movie.

The Dolls' first album would leave a huge impression on a powerful cult of fans, but unfortunately that loyalty didn't translate into big commercial sales. They were a hard sell for mainstream audiences. As one critic observed, "Their music is coarse, vulgar, simplistic, and loud. They wear makeup, lipstick, and six-inch high heels. They are the New York Dolls and you have to love rock 'n' roll to appreciate how beautiful they are."[7] They'd record one more album, aptly named *Too Much Too Soon*, and then implode in a glittery mess of addiction, ego, and bad timing. They had, however, helped to kick off a moment. Rock, which had always had its roots in the Molotov cocktail of sex and youth, was now increasingly pushing the borders of gender and glamour. The Age-of-Aquarius aspirations of the 1960s had not worked out for a lot of people, and in the shadow of Vietnam and Watergate they were ready for something different, whether it was the gritty subversion of punk or the feathery escapism of disco. In that aesthetic environment, the decade would bounce back and forth between the seriousness of social upheaval and the flash of nightlife—either way, beauty was ready for it.

In 1973, L'Oréal was looking for a way to pitch its beauty products to the modern woman when Ilon Specht, a copywriter at the powerful Madison Avenue firm of McCann Erickson, obliged with the deceptively simple tagline, "Because I'm Worth It." It was one small step for lipstick, one giant leap for womankind. With its bold declaration of self-worth and consumer feminism, L'Oréal had practically bottled the moment and set the standard for advertising to the me generation. It would be another year before women could hold credit cards without cosigning by their husbands,[†] but businesses quickly were realizing that a large part of women's liberation would rest in the financial freedom to pursue their own muses.

The women's movement of the 1960s had drawn some hard lines around makeup and the 1970s would both expand and soften them with messaging from both within and without the effort. House of Dior, for example, would launch a range of shades simply called "Feminism," under the tagline "It's So Liberating." "The woman today," the ads said, "Con-

---

† The Equal Credit Opportunity Act was passed in October 1974, and it "prohibits discrimination on the basis of race, color, religion, national origin, sex, marital status, or age in credit transactions." Anchored in some of her earlier legal wins for equity, its passage is often credited to the Notorious R.B.G., Ruth Bader Ginsburg.

fident, newly natural. She wants soft, muted colors that reflect fashion's new softness." Lipsticks came in Wild Coral Rose, Ivory Rose, Dusty Rose, and Smoky Rose, and as a promotion, the "If You Ever Need Me, Whistle on a Chain,"[8] which was hopefully just an accessory and not a warning about the rising crime rate and urban decay.

In mass media outlets, women seemed to be expressing a struggle to reconcile their desire for equity with self-expression and the consumer urge. In *Cosmopolitan*, writer Sara Davidson tried to square her ethics with a recent makeover, "How am I supposed reconcile all of this with the feminist philosophy that women shouldn't dress themselves as sex objects." Ultimately, she was willing to admit that there was something seductive about feeling good. "Rouge and lipstick. Fluffed up hair. Never had I felt so sleek and leggy. Never had I looked so perfect."[9] In synthesizing the lessons of feminism, beauty was now being redefined to be its own form of power beyond simply the ability to attract a suitable husband. To hear *Vogue* tell it, in the right lip gloss, you weren't merely a sex object, you were actively determining your own fate. As author of the article "Pretty: What It Means" explained, lipstick was "Self-respect, not dependency; selection, not sexual plumage. . . . This new sensibility is what sophistication should be all about."[10] This rebranding seemed to work, because while the Equal Rights Amendment would spend the decade being kicked back and forth as either the end of the American family as we knew it or the dawn of a shining new era of equality, the beauty industry recognized the need to play both sides of that fence.

Contemporary headlines claimed that "Women's Movement Boosts Cosmetics, Maker Says." The article explained that the "evidence was strong that working women use more makeup and other personal care products than housewives," further noting that 63 percent of all working women applied lipstick at least twice a day. According to one supplier of cosmetic cases, "I am certain that this concern of working women about their appearances leads them to use more beauty and personal care products never occurred to the leaders of the women's movement but nevertheless this is what happened."[11] The overemphasis on women's looks actually had been much on the minds of the women's movement leaders, and they'd been saying so expressly for years, but it's possible he'd missed that detail in tabulating his industry forecasts. This workplace pressure had also been occupying every waking thought of cosmetics executives, although their aims were quite different than those of the women's movement.

The future, experts predicted, lay in encouraging women to feel like they had made the right choices. In 1972, the niece of Mme. Helena Rubinstein and scion of the family business, Mala Rubinstein, was attuned to the moment and quick to point out some of the most famous feminists were not above a little primping. "Gloria Steinem's choice of tinted eyeglasses, for example, is not purely coincidental. The glasses, plus subtle makeup, are planned face decorations. The natural look Gloria projects is a projection of Liberation."[12]

This generous outlook may itself have been somewhat gendered, since, looking at the same circumstances and opportunities, the ever-cantankerous Charles Revson came away with a completely different impression. "Revson is an inveterate woman watcher," one 1972 article proclaimed, "It's all part of his female-oriented business and eventually he translated his impression-ideas into products." He somehow failed to see any potential profit in the fight for gender equity. "Gloria is a glorious looking girl with enough brains to twist words and ideologies to her advantage. Gloria has used the Lib movement as a personal vehicle to fame." Instead, he was banking on the appeal of women like Raquel Welch, "who breathed sexuality but didn't come on like gangbusters,"[13] and in his way, he was right. As the decade wore on, cultural pressure led women to tone down their opinions or risk being perceived as troublesome.

By the end of the decade, executives like Mala Rubinstein recognized that unalloyed feminism was losing its power and needed to be cloaked in something easier to swallow. Meaning that going forward, female wants and ambitions would have to be served up to the public in a stealthy way, like feeding a cheese-wrapped pill to a dog. This was especially true for working women; despite their all-time high numbers in the workforce, the office, factory, and sales floor were still a man's world, and women needed to learn how to function in it. "The fact is, Rubinstein says, is that there are fights for jobs. Women are always striving for recognition. The woman who gets ahead doesn't have to look like a man. The really fascinating woman thinks like a man and looks like a woman. That's feminism at its ideal." By combining "feminism, femininity,"[14] the thought was that lipstick could literally gloss over the hard truths women faced simultaneously earning a living and keeping up appearances. The popular lip color finish that year seemed to follow suit with a number of offerings that were shinier and less natural than ever, including the Rubinstein company's own "Brush-On Lips," an "ingenious new lipstick with a brush. Shines like a gloss, stays on like a lipstick."[15]

Even with these innovations and compromises, by 1977 even conservative wonk George F. Will clumsily contemplated how glamour and women's rights could coexist by posing the false equivalency, "Dolly Parton: biologically no woman is supposed to look like that and given the *Zeitgeist*, no woman is supposed to want to look like that."[16] What George had failed to consider was that although Dolly Parton had never publicly stated that she was a feminist, she also never said that she wasn't. In fact, she played into the bra-burning feminist myth by stating that her own demonstration "had taken the fire department three days to put out."[17] Moreover, if there was ever a woman who understood that dichotomous pressure of looking pretty and being taken seriously as a professional, it's Dolly.

Born to a poor family in Pittman Center, Tennessee, her music career alone boasts twenty-five *Billboard* number-one hits on the country music charts, fifty Grammy nominations, and a personal catalog of more than three thousand original songs—but none of that is probably first thing about her that comes to mind for most people. She's probably better known for her public persona, which she's carefully crafted from the best elements of guileless country girl, wise-cracking drag queen, large-hearted philanthropist, and skillful business tycoon. By the end of the 1970s, she'd already revamped her career trajectory several times over, smoothly (and smartly) transitioning from down-home girl singer to mainstream pop star who was about to launch into her first foray into movie stardom.

Announced in 1979, her debut film *9 to 5* would pair her with outspoken activists Lily Tomlin and Jane Fonda and play on the real-world tensions of working women for laughs. This was actually an incredibly brave move on Dolly's part, since at the time Jane Fonda's public image still was reeling from her militant opposition to the Vietnam War years earlier, and the association could have been troubling for core fans. "I can't think of two more dissimilar women than Jane Fonda and Dolly Parton, and yet I hear they're going to make a movie together," wrote one concerned fan on hearing of the production.[18] Superficially maybe, but in practice, Dolly was no less uncompromising in her career pursuits; she simply had mastered disguising her power in a curvy, blonde, rhinestone-studded package. Years before the Rubinsteins of the world had hit on combining "feminism, femininity," Dolly was already one of the twentieth century's great masters.

Part of this can be attributed to her Smoky Mountains upbringing, where glamour was not easy to come by and where she was "so poor a tube of lipstick was like a million dollars."[19] The one local role model she had was "the town tramp," whom her mother dismissed as "trash." Dolly later joked that it inspired an idea: "That's what I want to be when I grow up. I'm gonna be trash! And that is how I look." From a young age, she intuitively understood there was a certain sort of power in glamour and sex appeal, particularly if you were trying to hold your own in an industry dominated by men with Texas-sized egos. The result was a look that would last decades (and land her on the Worst Dressed list of 1978 and 1979): big hair, tight clothes, and lots of lipstick. The same year George F. Will was assessing her gravity, Barbara Walters went so far as to ask if she worried about being the butt of jokes. Dolly replied in the most "because I'm worth it" way by explaining that "Showbiz is a money-making joke and I always loved telling jokes." She would spend decades being dismissed as a novelty by those who never bothered to scratch the surface, but as the Reagan years dawned and consumerism overtook political conviction, she was able to capture (and cash in on) something that Rubinstein and Revson only guessed at: "A rhinestone shines just as good as a diamond." That is to say, artifice could be incredibly effective.

Dolly would shine on, but the glossy disco look and sound that had defined the era was dead. And not just dead but killed by an angry mob during a 1979 promotion for the Chicago White Sox called "Disco Demolition," which devolved into a full-on riot of angry rock fans who *Rolling Stone* characterized as "white males, eighteen to thirty-four are the most likely to see disco as the product of homosexuals, Blacks, and Latins, and therefore they're the most likely to respond to appeals to wipe out such threats to their security."[20] Ugly but not exactly shocking, it was a fitting end to a decade that had met social upheaval with numb pleasure seeking. Things were changing. Beverly Johnson became the first Black model to snag the cover of *Cosmo* in 1974, elements of gay culture were being mainstreamed, and a record number of women had entered the workforce. It was forward moving, but pushback was coming. The literal and figurative destruction of disco presaged the upcoming decade, which would usher in a new age of conformity and consumerism. A new wave was coming with the 1980s that drew inspiration from both the glamour of the past and the promise of the future, but it would bring with it the cultural recoil that followed AIDS, Reaganomics, the crack epidemic, and end of the Cold War.

CHAPTER TEN
GLOSSED IN SPACE
The 1980s

In 1982, the *LA Times* asked a bunch of fashion and beauty industry experts to reimagine what Nancy Reagan might look like if she were to get hip and ditch her fussy hair helmet and signature Chanel frocks. Executive editor Lew Harris said, "the remake was done because Mrs. Reagan is 'wrong for the eighties, too cold, too elitist'" and that according to their experts, a "(b)righter red lipstick will show up better in photographs and enliven the smile."[1] The resulting sketch renders her more suburban-mom-going-to-the-mall and less GOP power player. The suggestions failed to make even the slightest dent in her hairdo or her power suits. She already had chosen her team in the era's jocks-versus-nerds-versus-punks-versus-yuppies battles. She might not have been ready for the change, but a lot of Americans in the 1980s were ready for something entirely new—as long as it was retro. Stylistically, the era that bears her husband's name would be torn between a nostalgia for a past that had never really existed and a future that wasn't very appealing. The bold red lip would return for those on the cutting edge (Madonna, Grace Jones, Kim Basinger, and Cyndi Lauper) and soft pearly neutrals would be the go-to look for the play-it-safe establishment (Geraldine Ferraro, Princess Diana, Olivia Newton-John, and Cindy Crawford, but also for some reason, Adam Ant and several members of Poison).

Punk* had launched itself snarling and screaming into public consciousness around 1976 from the London and New York scenes, and by 1980 it had grown into a large enough monster to fester and mutate into its own subgenres and factions. Hardcore, postpunk, goth, new wave, psychobilly, Afropunk, Oi!, queercore, and others would emerge throughout the 1980s, each adding its own tribal fashion subtleties along the way (even though they were all *totally about the music, man!*). Male dominated but androgynous, hard but glamorous, new but retro, punk style would soon inject itself into mainstream fashion and express itself through makeup. By 1980 it was already walking the runways for the spring/summer collections and it was pronounced that "The fashion world is on the beat of boldly rouged cheeks and fuchsia lipstick and spiked heels with pointed toes."[2]

If any element of punk can be described as classic, the basics of the signature colorful cat eye and dark lipstick look can be traced to scenesters and musicians such as Soo Catwoman (née Sue Lucas), Jordan (née Pamela Rook), Siouxsie Sioux (née Susan Ballion), and Nina Hagen in Europe and Patricia Morrison (née Patricia Anne Rainone), Joan Jett (née Joan Marie Larkin), Poison Ivy Rorshach (née Kristy Wallace) and Debbie Harry (née Angela Trimble) in the United States. Being a do-it-yourself scene, there were of course infinite variations and those, like Patti Smith, who opted out entirely, but these are some of the iconic looks. The daring sexuality and darkness of red and black lipstick were near ubiquitous during the years when fashion magazines and advice columns were selling women bubblegum glosses and delicate pearl frosts.

Rooted in rebellion, the makeup twisted both what was conventionally expected of women and gave a middle finger to the quasi-feminist

---

* *Punk*, the magazine that gave the movement its name, was launched by writer Legs McNeil and cartoonist John Holmstrom in 1976 along with several cornerstone bands and albums. Punk as a word describing that rebellious sound and attitude can go back as far as the garage rock of the 1960s or rockabilly of the 1950s, depending on which music critic you ask.

natural look of the 1970s in order to create a spiky sort of glamour. As one *New York Times* writer summed up the play on good looks, "The singer . . . Debbie Harry, is a combination of Marilyn Monroe and Jack the Ripper. It wasn't meant to be appealing."[3]

Another aspect of the choose-your-own-adventure nature of punk style was that a lot of it came out of attics, fetish shops, home improvement centers, and thrift stores, which gave it a retro-futuristic look that was right for the moment. Reagan, with his dread of communists, convenient puritanism, and Brylcreem haircut, was himself a definite throwback to the 1950s. At the same time, the dawn of the consumer computer age was definitely upon us, with VCRs, microwaves, and Atari consoles being welcomed into every home. Thomas A. Greening, a psychologist observing 1980s worship of 1950s style, claimed that it was its own combination of punk and wishful thinking: "It's a rebellion against reality. . . . People need to create some other reality, some other mythic time that we think was easier, more pleasant, hipper. It may or may not have anything to do with what the fifties were actually like."[4]

The kitsch element and teenage rebellion narrative of rockabilly culture made it easy for punks to ditch mohawks for pompadours. Bands like the Stray Cats and the Blasters would cut a number of records and attract crowds that were happy to dress for the occasion. *Newsweek* captured the moment in 1983: "Traditional or original, they all sing of cars, girls, and parties to an addictive back beat. 'I feel like I'm in a time warp,' sighs 21-year-old Debbie Giglio pouffing her bouffant hairdo, replastering her ruby-red lipstick, and realigning her '50s strapless to suit her '80s cleavage."[5] No worries—if the bright reds of *I Love Lucy* weren't your speed, the decade also would cannibalize the pale creams of the '60s and the dark brick tones of the '40s at some point. For all of its space-age aspirations, the past was actually central to shaping the looks of the decade. That prolific nostalgia may also have had something to do with the global pressures of the present (e.g., nuclear proliferation, famine in Africa, hole in the ozone layer) that were making visions of the future somewhat dystopian.

Crammed between a technical revolution and a world in chaos, the popular culture was fairly obsessed with the notion of what would become of us in the future, and although the outlook for mankind was grim, the sartorial forecast was still pretty rocking. The female leads of *Escape from New York*, *Flash Gordon*, *Bladerunner*, and *Mad Max: Beyond*

Thunderdome all managed to maintain a classic, movie-star red lip in a prison colony, the planet Mongo, as a robot, and postapocalyptic Australia respectively. Consciously or not, this may also have been an area where the idea of the feminist "natural look" was still in play: sex objects stopped to primp, "strong female characters" ran like hell. Alien's Ellen Ripley and *Terminator's* Sarah Connor, for example, had places to go and creatures to kill and they did not have time for anything more than maybe a touch of nude gloss.

TV, on the other hand, was mainly fixed in the present and concerning itself with the upswing in the economy. Nighttime dramas such as *Dallas, Dynasty, Falcon Crest,* and *Knots Landing* ruled the ratings and featured plotlines that ranged from campy to crass about the lifestyles of the super-rich and ridiculously sexy. They were sexist, lowbrow, and totally nonsensical, and, naturally, 1980s audiences loved them.

Dynasty, in particular, with its Nolan Miller–designed, sequins-and-shoulder-pads fashions was an absolute consumer fantasy about what rich people did with their days. (Turns out, mainly doing nebulous "business" things, engaging in catfights, flying in private jets, having affairs, drinking champagne, and confronting long-lost relatives.) For the women of the show, the general look was an endless parade of furs, gowns, jewels, big hair, and bold lipstick choices; so much makeup, in fact, that they seemed to maintain their high-gloss lips and smoky eyes intact through mud fights, kidnappings, and car wrecks. It was such a cultural phenomenon that the producers tried (with mixed success) to merchandise every last element of it. In 1984, it was estimated that Americans bought $400 million in various *Dynasty*-themed odds and ends, including books, wallpaper, and pantyhose.[6] In a classic, Reagan-era story of overreach, the promised line of "beauty products from Charles of the Ritz"[7] never actually emerged, because the licensed clothing was an expensive flop and interest was waning.

Separates with linebacker-sized shoulders and a profusion of sequins somehow never caught on with women. Although over-the-top glamour is fun to watch on television, the line was actually quite pricey and a flashy fashion statement that was difficult to work into an everyday wardrobe for working women and suburban moms.[8] It does, however, stand as an important business lesson for future licensees of cosmetics from rock stars to couturiers: start with the affordable lipsticks and perfumes and work your way up from there—not the other way around.†

If soap opera–inspired fashions failed to catch on, it wasn't because the zeitgeist was experiencing a minimalist moment. The young urban professional—or yuppie—was the archetype of the moment and they were (for better or worse) driving the culture toward a shameless embrace of conspicuous consumerism that obnoxiously announced that they had arrived. White collar, college educated, and flush with cash (or at least a high credit rating), they were portrayed in mass media as wanting the newest and the best. For men this meant power ties and Porsches; for women, designer labels would now be worn on the outside and placed on everything from linens to lipsticks.

This new emphasis on luxury and "Because I'm Worth It" indulgence would translate perfectly into lipstick sales. Even though the first two years of the 1980s were marked by hangover inflation from the 1970s oil crisis, the beauty industry was looking forward to a boom time. Sales volume may have been decreasing, but the margins were increasing, and that was good news for profits. If it was bad news for consumers, the industry didn't sweat it—it was feeling bulletproof. One industry analyst suggested makeup was now a necessary step in women's daily routines and not one that they felt comfortable scrimping on or going without. "Today cosmetics are not a luxury, but a part of a person's dress and their face to the world." One manufacturer claimed that beauty was just part of the cost of doing business, declaring that "There's always a need for something that will make a person attractive."[9]

This would prove especially true for working women who were continuing to adhere to the dress-for-success narrative, especially now that they were impossibly busy climbing the corporate ladder. Women were starting to push away from the soft, tomboyish *Annie Hall* and *Bonnie and Clyde* looks that had marked the 1970s and were starting to think about how to balance femininity and dressing professionally. "'Let's be realistic,' says a woman in investment banking. 'no one is ever going to forget I'm

---

† Among the people who picked up on this wisdom was Alexis Carrington Colby herself. Dame Joan Collins launched her own line of lipsticks, skin care, and fragrances in 2014. It's called "Timeless Beauty" and is aimed at women of a certain age in the United Kingdom.

a woman, so why should my clothes deny my gender. There's nothing wrong with being competent and attractive.'"[10] In fact, it was pretty much a requirement. The same article suggested that women should "Keep a good mirror in your desk and make it a habit to touch up with powder, blusher, and lipstick at lunchtime. You'll look perfect all day."[11] The message hadn't changed much since magazines were coaching Depression-era gals in the steno pool: it wasn't enough to be good at your job, you had to look flawless doing it.

Plus, in this fast-paced world, it wasn't just "making up" anymore, it was, as *Vogue* put it, "time invested." You were always on the go and your day should begin with "Two minutes . . . to find the perfect flash of new lip color (what we've discovered here, is Orlane's Mandarin-red Cornaline.) It's real color, not glaring—and that's the new look of this spring."[12] Revlon's "Wall Street Violets" was probably a good choice for those in the finance world.

Of course, this advice all presumed that women were in white-collar office positions, where they had the time, money, and flexibility to do their makeup, which was truer than it had been for a segment of professional women, but not nearly the big picture. The number of women in the workforce had doubled since the 1950s, but more than 80 percent of the positions were still pink collar, "The women who type the letters and file the papers, wait on tables, sell the clothes, clean the houses and offices, empty the bed pans, dish out the food in cafeterias, run the sewing machines, put the lipstick in the cases and tuna in cans."[13] These women were, of course, also expected to look good at all times, and there would be any number of mass market brands that were willing to cater to them in drugstores and five-and-dimes; in the fantasy world of fashion magazines, however, the sky was the limit in terms of income spent and "time invested."

Literally the sky for some working women. When NASA announced in 1983 that it would send Sally Ride as a crew member of an upcoming shuttle mission, the style questions began to fly. This was also a matter of national pride: Dr. Ride wasn't the first woman in space—the Soviet Union's Valentina Tereshkova, "a dimpled bachelor girl who wore lipstick into space"[14] held that distinction—but as an American woman she was expected to make an appropriate splash. Dr. Ride—a PhD in physics, championship tennis player, and professor of nonlinear optics—ultimately decided she had other more pressing concerns in the dark void of space and opted for a "mascaraless shuttle ride." In doing so, she opted to leave behind the specially curated "female preference kit," which included "'Icy Blue' eye shadow and 'Rose' blush by Revlon, Prince Matchabelli black-brown mascara and eyeliner, pressed face powder, lip gloss and makeup remover."[15] The original kit, which was never actually launched, is now a part of the Smithsonian's permanent collection. Other kits probably did make the trek, as one wire service noted, "Revlon may have its day in space yet. There are seven other women waiting in the wings to fly in space, and some, like Rhea Seddon, will use the female preference kit. Said Seddon: 'Others are perfectly gorgeous without it, but I myself like to put a little lipstick on in the morning.'"[16] Seddon, the Ruth Elder of outer space, would make three trips on the shuttles *Discovery* and *Columbia* beginning in 1985; an MD, she also packed a bone saw to do equipment repairs.

Meanwhile back on Earth, a twist in technology meant that there now would be some male professionals who would be actively encouraged to wear makeup along with a new way to market to women. Specifically, the nationwide advent of cable TV and the 1981 launch of MTV meant that popular music was now more of a visual medium than ever. For a few cagey artists, this would translate into an all-out strategic assault on gender norms with startlingly different reactions. It was a winning formula from the beginning, with manufacturers almost immediately adapting to give young audiences what they wanted. Even formerly staid, ladylike companies rushed to follow the androgyny trend, and by 1985, everyone was making MTV-like videos. "'Let's face it. They [videos] are today' says Leslie Weller, public relations director for Elizabeth Arden, Inc. 'Our fall promotion of New Wave cosmetics was directly inspired by MTV and that whole mood.'"[17] If young women wanted a shade they had seen in a video, it just made good business sense to give it to them. "With the average age of the rock video viewer now estimated to be 24 and the average income of a viewing household to be $31,000,‡ it's no wonder the fashion business is taking note of the whole thing. Some of a fashion retailer's best customers fit the same profile."[18]

In these olden days when music was still central to MTV's programming, new wave artists (and its style cousin, the new romantics) were

---

‡ That's about $80,000 in 2021 dollars. Definitely yuppie territory.

among the first to make it big on the new channel with their postpunk English cool and natural understanding of costuming. Bands like Duran Duran, Culture Club, Depeche Mode, and Adam and the Ants swept in on a bright cloud of smash cuts and lip gloss and were a near-instant hit with teen girls (and some boys). Whereas the New York Dolls had been pilloried for their use of spandex and cosmetics, this new generation would be deemed to be bubbly and sexually harmless enough to be seen as cute—eventually. This is partly attributable to the fact that the packaging was just slicker, and the times had changed ever so slightly. By 1984, even Adam Ant (né Stuart Goddard) was amazed how far audiences had come. "It's no longer a big deal, when a guy wears makeup in public. Now, when I wore lipstick and nail polish on 'Good Morning America' in 1980, that caused quite a fuss."[19] This was sweet, but not exactly the whole truth—the era was indeed slightly more tolerant than it had been, but not entirely ready to embrace equality or difference. This was, after all, at the beginning of the AIDS epidemic, and the nation was suffering from a virulent and collective homophobia that plagued every aspect of life from the Reagan administration to rock 'n' roll.

Boy George, in particular, required a lot of explaining and whether that was positive or negative depended on who was doing the explication. Some understood that makeup was part of the performance. "The face is nearly as ubiquitous as Michael Jackson's, if slightly less exotic, framed by swatches of long hair and beribboned braids, and glossed by generous applications of blusher, eyeshadow, mascara and carmine lipstick. It's clearly a face designed to confuse, to captivate, and above all to attract attention to its owner, Mr. George Alan O'Dowd."[20] To others, it was a violation of the sex symbol/rock star code that bad boys like Elvis Presley (in lots of mascara), Jimi Hendrix (a fan of feather boas), and Mick Jagger (where to even start?) had lived and swaggered by. One author's "Boy George Theory" had makeup as a sign of mental illness gone unchecked.

> Boy George is from England and his name is George O'Dowd and he sings with a group called Culture Club and he dresses just like a girl, makeup, lipstick, ribbons in the hair, the whole bit. In an earlier time in this country, mental health authorities would have been alerted had there been a male person wandering around singing in his sister's clothes. But that has changed now. Boy George has made enough

money to keep himself in Cover Girl and eyeshadow the rest of his life, performing to sellout crowds of screaming children, who should be doing their homework.[21]

The suggestion seemed to be that little girls should grow up and find themselves manlier rockers, perhaps like the spandex-clad men of hair metal.

Artists could get away with a certain amount of theatrical makeup and crazy outfits if the songs were about strippers and the guitar solos took half an hour. "It is an album cover Max Factor would have loved. . . . Each of the four wears lipstick and foundation makeup. . . . Clearly, the four old pros are in the powder-and-paint game. And just who are these people? High-fashion models? Some of those tootsies you see traipsing through music videos? Heck, no, it's just the guys in Poison."[22] See? Nothing to worry about here in terms of sexual mores or gender lines, just a successful band from the Sunset Strip's thriving metal scene. Critics were quick to recognize that with these performers their lipstick-wearing was purely theatrical. "From Poison, with their tight, brightly colored Spandex outfits, dandelion haircuts, and feminine makeup to Mötley Crüe, whose clothes and makeup suggest a sort of commedia dell'arte from hell, glam's now rock's most outrageous look right now. No wonder Aerosmith sent the scene up with its hit 'Dude Looks Like a Lady.'"[23] Every rose may have its thorn and every trend (no matter how chart topping) has its expiration date, so by the end of the decade, even metal and punk rocked a more stripped-down, jeans-and-flannel look, and lipstick was reserved for the women spinning out dance-floor anthems (and maybe the occasional goth guy).

The 1980s were ultimately a mix of glamour and cruelty; the haves had more (and we applauded) and the have-nots had less (and, on some level, we blamed them for it), all of which played itself out in politics, culture, and beauty. The rise of increasingly segmented prestige brands such as Clinique, Lancôme, and Fashion Fair meant that there was a lipstick for every outfit, identity, and attitude. The look was about decadence and declaring your lifestyle to the world at large, whether it was a subtle Chanel lipstick on an up-and-coming female professional or hot pink gloss on a video vixen. It was a moment that would have long-term effects on both the way we bought makeup for ourselves and what it meant to step over the boundaries of self-expression. Going into the 1990s, the look might have been more down to earth but it still made a statement, and technology would open even more channels for buying, selling, and declaring ourselves to the world.

CHAPTER ELEVEN

SMELLS LIKE TEEN LIPSTICK
The 1990s

Shades of the Decade
MAC Viva Glam
Urban Decay Gash
Chanel Vamp
L'Oréal Real Raisin
Bobbi Brown Pale Pink

Punk, metal chick, yuppie, fly girl—whatever a woman's look during the 1980s, the big hair, stirrup pants, and elaborate makeup was a lot of work. It's no wonder that the 1990s look was going to be something a bit more unplugged. It's as if as a society we collectively decided we were ready to be a bit more casual. We elected our first baby boomer president, embraced baggy jeans, and bought unisex fragrances. That was on the surface. At its heart, *Harper's Bazaar* summed up the matte browns, dark reds, and glossy pink–driven look of the decade as "carefully contrived minimalism."[1] The era that fully embraced grunge and girl power was ready to work hard at looking like it had just rolled out of bed. From Courtney Love's smear of scarlet to Paris Hilton's adolescent pink gloss, women of the 1990s were going to spend a lot of time, money, and effort to declare themselves, but in a way that made the gesture seem spontaneous. Going into the digital age our relationship with lipstick could best be described as "It's complicated."

Greasy, dirty, edgy, and unkempt—as a look grunge had a certain do-it-yourself (DIY) democracy to it. In 1993, it also got no less than ten pages in *Vogue*, which featured (among other things) Naomi Campbell draped in gauzy Anna Sui frocks. Not quite metal, not quite punk, it was the antidote to the 1980s overkill and was soon as much of a fashion statement as a sound. Makeup-wise, it generally meant sparse eyebrows, pale skin, and dark lips. It wasn't exactly the deliberate statement of punk or the sex-kitten appeal of glam, but it wasn't nothing, either. The fashion of rolling out into the world in baggy flannels and Dr. Martens boots was supposed to appear coolly indifferent and antifashion, but it also had a certain kind of cache. *Vogue* declared it a casual insurgency, writing, "Throw out your detergent. This is not a call to arms; it's an invitation to dress down and party up! As the fin de siècle draws near, greed has gone to seed. What started out as a serf's rebellion against aristocratic glamour has turned into a fashion revolution that champions 'revolting' for its own sake."[2]

So it wasn't exactly deep but it wasn't entirely empty, either, since a new sort of popular feminism would emerge from the music underground sporting a red lip and a serious attitude problem. Drawing from a fresh body of mainstream feminist writings such as Susan Faludi's *Backlash* and Naomi Wolf's *The Beauty Myth* and their own shared information network of zines, there was a new school of thought that suggested that makeup in and of itself wasn't the enemy. The riot grrrl emerged from the underground ready to reclaim the totems of womanhood on her own terms (and rock out). A new generation of political punks, these young women took their sexuality, sexual agency, and their outfits very seriously, no matter how threadbare or eclectic. Often scrawling words like "slut" and "whore" on their bodies as a way of reclaiming toxic language, they paired femininity with righteous rock star anger.

The *Washington Post* tried to capture the look in the moment, explaining how it built on the tough-girl punk model of Patti Smith and Exene Cerenka: "The Riot Grrrl style, though, also allows girls to add traditional styles of femininity to the new identity. Courtney Love of the band Hole adopts a kind of kindergarten whore approach in her dress, all ribbons and lace with bleach blonde hair and smeared red lipstick."[3] Love got a lot of attention—partly due to her marriage to Nirvana front man Kurt Cobain, partly due to her drug-addled behavior, which included constant scrapping with other musicians, and partly due to her actual musical output—but she wasn't the first or last of her kind in the alt-rock world. Bands like Bratmobile, L7, Babes in Toyland, and Bikini Kill all added their own styles to the movement. That said, in 1996, the trend-predicting *American Forecaster Almanac* was ready to call grunge DOA, telling the Associated Press that "grunge will fade away in the new year. As will bright red lipstick."[4] This was partially true, grunge may have run its course, but as history has shown, red lipstick never quite goes away entirely.

Like many subcultures, a lot was lost in translation in attempting to mainstream grunge and riot grrrl and within just a couple of years of becoming a style that could be sold at junior's boutiques, "Riot Grrrls [were] no longer angry feminists but sassy babes with funny outfits."[5] Altogether, it lasted a short time with a limited number of actual players, but it was an influential moment that would have a long-lasting effect on how Generation X viewed lipstick and feminism as entirely compatible and one that made a lasting impression on the people in charge of marketing to that segment of the population. They learned new lessons in how to quantify things like rebellion, self-expression, and sexuality as part of their sales plan. By the end of the decade, the core of this DIY feminism would mutate in the mainstream into a couple catchphrases, namely "do me feminism" (a phrase coined by a male *Esquire* writer), which divorced sex positivity from any need for social justice or economic parity. It was a male fantasy of empowerment and mercifully didn't last long, since it was mostly featured in men's magazine spreads where "You will find a lot of big hair and lipstick and arty-looking women posing in sheets or lolling about in tight t-shirts." On the other end of the spectrum was "girl power," which—despite all the baggage of consumer feminism—has left a surprisingly deep impact with its ability to make gender equity adorable and easily digested when paired with everything from the Spice Girls to the Women's March.

If the 1980s opened the door to street fashion as high fashion, the 1990s walked right in and looted whatever was left. Hip-hop, skater chic, club kids, goth, low-rider culture, swing dancing, and the rave scene were all strip-mined for the next big thing. Even drag would emerge from the underground for its moment in the spotlight. With women's power on the rise, a generation of sexually active people grappling with AIDS, and a culture questioning the status quo of white and male, the moment was especially right for gender play. Twenty years after it had denounced "fag rock," even the *Boston Globe* acknowledged a shift.

> Gays and lesbians are gaining visibility, bisexuality is a twentysome-
> thing trend, AIDS is stifling everyone with fear. Our private sexual
> identity inquiries are being mirrored in our media. For many viewers,
> drag queens and kings are adored images of power and individuality: "I
> am what I am, I am my own special creation," goes the anthem from
> the Broadway musical "La Cage Aux Folles." Gender players appear to
> have freed themselves from the narrow social rules and roles that are
> confounding everyone else. They are also emblems of triumph over the
> body's limitations.[6]

Enter RuPaul Charles. Emerging from New York's infamous club scene, RuPaul managed the near-impossible by turning his drag persona into a household name through smart career choices and sheer personal charisma. Starting in 1993 with the release of his undeniable dance hit "Supermodel (You Better Work)," RuPaul launched a charm offensive on the American public that culminated with him being named the first openly gay, Black, nongender-conforming spokesmodel for a major cos-metics line in 1995 for MAC's Viva Glam lipstick.

It was a bold and savvy choice on the part of MAC (short for Makeup Artist Cosmetics), which was—at the time—an up-and-coming boutique brand with an edgy catalog of colors, editorial props, and a celebrity following. The casting was just splashy enough to be headline grab-bing without being alienating or controversial and—as a fundraiser for AIDS—altruistic enough to avoid cynicism. The Viva Glam campaign paired RuPaul with singer k.d. lang, then one of the few out butch lesbi-ans in entertainment with a velvety voice and a denim personal style. For many Americans, it was their first introduction to the spectrum of ways that people play with gender; lang signed on precisely because she under-stood the impact of the imagery, saying in 1996, "It's so odd that their idea of a spokesperson would include a drag queen, a Black drag queen. It's so outrageous. And their idea of a second spokesperson is someone who doesn't wear makeup. That intrigues me. It's rebellious and it's pro-gressive."[7] As for RuPaul, he too was aware of what his over-the-top look was putting out. "'The message, honey, is that everyone can be beautiful,' Ru told reporters at the campaign launch. 'I've been wearing MAC for five years now and look at me—I'm a big, old Black man under all this makeup, honey, and if I can be beautiful, so can you.'"[8] It was a message of positivity and inclusion that worked, making RuPaul a household name and America's unofficial ambassador of drag, launching MAC's makeup empire into the stratosphere and raising millions for the fight against HIV/AIDS.*

The exponential growth of MAC in these years was emblematic of a trend that had begun to flourish in the 1980s but had existed for years before that: prestige brands. A number of women were now in a position in which they easily could be convinced to spend top dollar on their lipsticks for reasons beyond the appeal of flaunting designer labels. This growth translated into a boom in the sheer number of brands and the increasing segmentation of the market. Cosmetics manufacturers would not only sell you the red or nude or blue you wanted, but included free with purchase a little bit of your lifestyle with it as well. Whether you viewed yourself as young and trendy, simple and sophisticated, earthy and easy, or continental and classic, there was a brand that matched your sense of style (that was, in turn, probably owned by a larger corporate conglomerate like Estée Lauder or L'Oréal, which might not be to your taste). A lot of this growth can be attributed to baby boomers, who had grown up being marketed to and felt at home declaring their worth and their lifestyle's specialness, and to their Gen X kids, who wanted their own innovative brands. Coincidentally, this was all happening at the same time that celebrity beauty culture started to rise, thereby creating perfect conditions for a new generation of tastemakers.

Like Max Factor decades before, makeup artists like Carol Shaw, Kevyn Aucoin, and Bobbi Brown would become almost as famous as the faces they painted and would build their own successful, high-end brands based on the star looks they helped to shape. Bridging the 1980s supermodel fad with 1990s celebrity culture, they appeared in dozens of magazines posing alongside their famous clients, offering cute insider anecdotes, and giving on-trend advice, which enabled them to build the

---

* Since its launch in 1994, MAC's Viva Glam lipsticks have raised more than $500 million for the MAC Viva Glam Fund. After Ru and k.d., the company continued to feature entertainers, including a number of groundbreaking female artists including Mary J. Blige, Cyndi Lauper, Lady Gaga, and more, in addition to two cis gay men, Elton John and Ricky Martin.

sort of cache that attracts the financial and name-recognition capital one needs to successfully launch a brand. These were no mere technicians; these were modern-day star makers who knew secrets that you didn't.

- In *Vogue*: Kevyn's hands have glorified every face from Audrey Hepburn's to Demi Moore's to Tina Turner's. He gave Janet Jackson her now signature "golden" look then took her space wild for this year's *Scream* video (Jackson won't leave home without him). Now Aucoin is booked for magazines, advertising, and publicity work months in advance and has a day rate in the thousands of dollars.[9]

- In *Redbook*: Want skin like Nicole Kidman's? Lips like Kim Basinger's? Makeup artist Carol Shaw has the inside story on Hollywood's beautiful faces. Meg Ryan, Geena Davis, Nicole Kidman, and Demi Moore have more in common than hot screen careers: each also has a uniquely glamorous look that relies at least in part on LA makeup artist Carol Shaw and her own special line of (Lorac) cosmetics.[10]

- In *Harper's Bazaar*: Beauty secrets are what beauty editors live for. If it's happening backstage, behind the scenes, on the set, we want to know about it. This is why we're happy to report makeup artist Bobbi Brown's new book *Bobbi Brown Beauty* (HarperCollins), a compilation of everything from working with top models, celebrities, fashion designers, and photographers. . . . Our favorite chapter (not surprisingly) is Beauty Trade Secrets.[11]

It was expertise you could acquire. These lines meant that even if you couldn't live like a celebrity on your salary, you could still purchase a little piece of the dream. Even a top-shelf lipstick always has been a relatively accessible way to live the fantasy.

Thanks to the internet, in the next few years what constituted a celebrity, or a makeup artist for that matter, would shift radically. But before the pop stars and influencers cut out the middlemen and started their own lines, the celebrities and their makeup artists could make or break a color trend. Where they got their ideas was a conversation that would come later. Pop star Gwen Stefani, for example, would blend the sacred with subculture signifiers without a thought to the deeper meanings, such as South Asian and Latinx items, specifically, "a blend of Los Angeles street styles—thrift-store glam, Mexican chola, Hollywood punk rock, and wild card bindi." The Mexican-inspired look in particular often would take the form of a dark, sharp lip line and pale or markedly darker lip. It was part of a larger style that was significant to female gang members for its hard-edged glamour and tribal sense of belonging. It was one of a number of trends picked up and discarded from vulnerable populations without proper context or attribution. Stefani, Madonna, and others would lift a look whole cloth, rendering it detached, harmless, and disposable. The beauty industry would take a while to have the hard conversations surrounding what was inspiration and what was appropriation when taking from people of color, but at least inclusion had begun to enter the industry's consciousness.

Latina women in particular were entering the conversation as they became a segment of the population that was growing but still underserved in a lot of areas. Christie Haubegger, the publisher of *Latina* magazine, saw the opportunity for brands with the vision to court this $350 billion and growing market. Explaining that her "readers are so excited someone's talking to them. 'You think I'm important? You want to sell me lipstick? Wow, thanks.' For a long time, we've been like kids with our noses up against the glass."[12] Beauty companies were among the first to realize that there was money to be made for speaking directly to this segment of the population—sort of. Rather than cast an actual Latina model for targeted ads, Revlon simply gave supermodel Cindy Crawford "a Latin look in an ad for dark shades of Revlon lipstick in the premiere issue of *Latina*, a bilingual magazine targeted at Hispanic women."[13] Progress would be a process.

Representation in the form of Latinx-owned beauty businesses and executives, like those at Besame and Beautyblender, would increase in the coming decades, but in the meantime major players would have to learn to talk to the Latinx market. Money was being left on the table according to *Vogue* writer Nely Galán. Latina stars were on the rise in 1997 with Salma Hayek, Cameron Diaz, and Jennifer Lopez all getting major movie roles and "despite the fact that nearly half the 27 million Latinos living in this country are women, barely a single company has targeted this market aggressively. . . . No wonder the first question out of mouth with a fellow Latina is 'What lipstick are you wearing?'"[14] No longer content to be an afterthought in the beauty world, women of color were demanding to see themselves represented both in the magazines that they read and the shades that they bought. Fortunately, companies were slowly but surely beginning to expand their shade range and to add a handful more non-white models.

By the end of the decade not only was the messaging of the beauty industry changing, the way in which people purchased cosmetics was about to get an overhaul. In 1998, the French open-stock chain Sephora opened its first U.S. location, which would be a game changer for the beauty industry and for a generation of shoppers who were no longer religiously brand loyal and relied on their own opinions over the expertise of sales reps at department stores or boutiques. The high-end, shop-for-yourself format eventually received such a huge response that major retailers like Macy's would experiment with its own floor space and chains like Ulta would spring up nationwide. The other factor, of course, was the internet.

Like nearly every other business (except maybe porn), beauty initially wasn't sure how to translate its real-world model into a virtual one. Clinique made itself an early, if awkward, adopter by offering a unique gift at its retail counters: "Talk about in-your-face marketing. Clinique is betting that the way to getting more women on line is by offering a smear of Internet information along with lipsticks and lotions. Since July 1, Clinique's Women's Guide to the Internet is free for the asking at any of its counters. It includes a copy of Netscape's Navigator 2.0 for Windows, a trial account on Netcom Online service and a 10-page plain-English guide to getting on line."[15] The guide, of course, directed female users to www.clinique.com.

Getting women online was actually a huge part of the equation. In 1995 the internet accounted for less than 2 percent of all beauty sales and though it was predicted to "eclipse $10 billion by the year 2000,"[16] the trick to building sales was getting a critical mass of women to this untested new platform. As trade bible *Women's Wear Daily* laid it out, "The lack of being able to touch and sniff is acknowledged to be a big barrier for selling beauty via computer. Another obstacle has been surfing the Net is still more highly favored by men—the wrong gender when it comes to building an audience for beauty marketing."[17] Beauty companies would figure it out, stepping in gently at first as a purely informational outlet offering tips, tricks, and news of their latest launches. That same year, *Harper's Bazaar* asked experts what they predicted, and some of them had a hard time envisioning the two-dimensional offerings of the web translating to the three-dimensional world of cosmetics. According to Maria Gomez, head of public relations for Bloomingdale's Miami, the future—as she envisioned it—was for what you already knew worked.

> "It will be tricky because cosmetics are such personal items." Brand loyalty, she believes, will allow cosmetic companies to thrive on-line.[†] "People will buy their tried-and-true favorites whether they're available in the store or on-line. But, of course, unless computers become incredibly sense-oriented, you'll still have to come into the store to touch, feel, and smell the new products."[18]

We now know that she was adorably, crushingly wrong, but it was a reasonable guess based on the way women had consumed lipstick until that moment.

Ironically (and the 1990s were really into irony), the ascendance of the internet—along with a host of real-world factors—would mark the decline of both the department store and the suburban mall as the places to go for makeup. The turn of the century would usher the world into the internet era and give rise to a new golden age for beauty, celebrity (and infamy), and expertise. Plus, an entirely new creature was born from all of these things rolled into one—the influencer. But before that, the explosion in brands, the easy access to information, and the worship of fame eventually would change the way lipstick was advertised. The Estée Lauder company gave an inkling of what was to come when it chose actress Elizabeth Hurley as the face of the brand in 1995. Hurley was not a model-turned-actress in the conventional sense as Andie MacDowell and Isabella Rossellini had been. At that moment she was almost exclusively an actress yet not really a well-known movie star in the same way that Max Factor's studio players were or Catherine Deneuve for Chanel was. In the United States, where Lauder was headquartered, she was re-

---

† Like lipstick, online evolved as a word through usage. In the mid-1990s the act of being on the World Wide Web was spelled out by various publications as on line, on-line, and online.

143

ally more of a celebrity for having worn a scant, safety pin–embellished Versace dress to the premiere of her then-boyfriend Hugh Grant's movie *Four Weddings and a Funeral* in 1994. She was, if you will, famous for being famous and in really good shape.

Whatever her qualifications, she was soon explaining her new career move to the *New York Times*. "'It's quite weird. I've never modeled before. You have to concentrate every moment. Every shot it important. They want to sell a million lipsticks,' she went on. 'It's a different skill than acting. We're selling, which I've never done before.'"[19] She was right; she was also an innovator. Liz Hurley had rolled out the red carpet for the next generation of celebrity spokespeople. In the new millennium there would be the sisters Hilton, Kardashian, Jenner, and others selling the fantasy beauty, sex appeal, and wealth that always had come along with lipstick, not because they were well-known models, accomplished actresses, or even career women, but because they were well-connected, conventionally attractive, and (almost more importantly) had an existing media following. The era of the prefab celebrity had arrived along with dial-up internet access.

CHAPTER TWELVE
THE YOU TUBE
The New Millennium

Shades of the Decades
MAC Ruby Woo
Kylie Cosmetics Lip Kit in Kristen
Huda Beauty Liquid Lipsticks in Trophy Wife
Pat McGrath Matte Trance in Antidote
Clinique Almost Lipstick in Black Honey

In the popular imagination, the twenty-first century was the *future*. If you believed in science fiction's brightest vision, the look was going to be sleek, silver, and cool. Sadly, when that shining (or apocalyptic) future became the present, there were no everyday jetpacks or tractor beams. In the absence of space travel, however, there was the internet, which would have an incalculable effect on the way we consumed and communicated in the coming decades. In the newly minted information age, if we were not exactly about social progress, we were crazy about speed: higher bandwidth, faster fashion, and a rapid churn of celebrity news. All of which would, in turn, impact the hot new colors, finishes, and brands of lipstick. Eventually—first the market had to deal with the real-world consequences of terrorism and economic uncertainty.

Tossing aside the matte browns and deep berries of the grunge era, the look of 2000 ushered in sheer, glossy reds. Even *Ladies' Home Journal* announced a new era for the old favorite. "Red lipstick is hot, hot, hot again, but the modern way to wear it is translucent and soft."[1] Also back in a big way—the male gaze. According to *Cosmo*, "'Matte red lips are no longer the signature seductive makeup maneuver. What's in now is a bright orangey red, soaking-wet lip look that's in your face sexy,'" says NYC makeup artist Paco Blancas. "'But don't expect a guy to look you in the eye when you're wearing this fiery effect—one glance and your mouth will become the center of his universe.'"[2] The moment may have been sexier, but it wasn't exactly decadent either. Puffed up by an overvalued IT sector, the economy itself was doing a delicate bubble dance that was about to go boom.

By 2001 investors were beginning to recognize that there wasn't a gold mine behind every dot-com address and the market had begun to bleed. Fall of that year would drain the rest of the dot-com bubble. More than a tragedy, 9/11 was a cultural turning point. It tanked the markets, crushed the nation's sense of security, and demanded a national moment of self-reflection. *Vanity Fair*'s editor, E. Graydon Carter, famously observed, "There's going to be a seismic change. I think it's the end of the age of irony."[3] Which, ironically, was way off the mark. We were America, damn it, and we didn't want seriousness; we wanted a new era of fast fashions, people who were famous for being famous, and the nonstop train wreck of reality TV. Sure, we would have to adjust to the new economy and take our shoes off at the airport, but we wouldn't let the terrorists win by changing our buying habits. We hadn't slowed down lipstick consumption for the fascists of World War II or the commies of the Cold War, and we weren't going to do it for the war on terror, either.

Despite a difficult economy, cosmetics were doing pretty well, including the luxury end of the market. One executive tried to keep it positive, saying in *Women's Wear Daily*, "One important bright spot for our entire industry is the perception of fine fragrance and cosmetics are affordable luxuries. That said, the tough economy instills a sense of caution in terms of spending, so consumers are look for high-quality and high-value of-ferings."[4] The concept of consumers flocking to little luxuries during recessions would be crystalized by (or at least attributed to) Estée Lauder chairman, Leonard Lauder, and dubbed the "lipstick index" by market watchers. It's become a favorite chestnut of the popular press during times of economic downturn; however, the problem is that it isn't at all accurate as an indicator. Lipstick spending goes up in good times as well as lean ones, so although seemingly logical, there's no actual, mathematical correlation between cosmetic sales and the ups and downs of the economy.

Amid the new landscape of the internet, 9/11, and a wobbly economy, cosmetics companies were trying to find the most effective message in a world that seemed to be spinning slightly off its usual axis. With no singular zeitgeist, the only way to go was trial and error. Avon, for example, after years of being the choice of suburban moms, knew it was looking a little dowdy and wanted to get with the times. It kicked off Y2K with its first female CEO and a $30 million investment in its website, which was meant to lift stagnant sales from traditional Avon ladies.[5] It also tried physical stores, called Avon Centers, casting customers as spokesmodels[6] and spinning out a new brand called "mark.," which was aimed at teenage girls.[7] As it had been since the 1950s, chasing the teen dollar was a smart move for companies seeking to improve revenue. Interestingly, though teens were increasingly brand and trend savvy as consumers, mark. offered only sheer lip colors and nothing in the red family until several years after its launch.

Cover Girl, Revlon, and Lancôme agreed that changes were needed and reexamined their approaches to younger consumers in the hopes of adding to their loyal customer base and refreshing their brands' overall looks. Sometimes the changes were subtle, like Lancôme minimizing its signature rose logo, because it was "kind of dated," according to their brand strategist.[8] Sometimes the changes were more complex. Cover Girl, for example, went the route that had been so successful for MAC by pairing celebrity and charity. They enlisted Queen Latifah and encouraged young consumers to give to charities by attaching altruism to star power. "Cover Girl has long sponsored programs to encourage young women to get involved in charitable causes. But, no matter how heartfelt, this is a hard way to get teenagers to buy more lipstick. So, in an attempt to be cool instead of sappy, Cover Girl is reinforcing its 'look good, be good' message with music fresh off the CD burner."[9] Revlon skipped the philanthropy and went straight to the celebrity, hiring model-of-the-moment James King and actress Halle Berry for its ads.

It was a reasonable move; fame had moved product since Lillian Russell had endorsed the offerings of Parfumerie Monte Carlo in the nineteenth century. As America modernized and movie stars became household gods, they became the arbiters of glamour and beauty and their faces could be used to create demand. Same with TV, radio, and almost every other mass media we invented and adopted. It was a fine formula: mass media created fame and fame sold lipstick. So why should the internet be any different? In function, it wasn't; in form, it was a huge change. Between the internet, smartphones, and high-speed connections, the ability to produce and consume information was getting faster and going further than ever before. Not only were there endless options for entertainment and retail, but users could create and distribute their own content and launch their own fads. The zine culture of the 1990s became the blogosphere of the early 2000s, which would in turn become the influencers of the 2010s.

This was going to be a game changer for lipstick. As early as 2004, the high-end beauty PR firm DeVries Public Relations declared in the industry staple *Women's Wear Daily* that its worth in the field was its unique ability to "create the buzz that builds business. Our programs include the widest spectrum of media and focus on influencer marketing."[10] The neologism *influencer* was barely (if at all) present in the public consciousness and the savvier members of the industry already were hunting down bloggers who had figured out how to build their own followings. This was still the era of Yahoo groups and MySpace; Facebook had launched the same year, but it was still mostly for students. YouTube wouldn't emerge until 2005, and Instagram in 2010.

A new hybrid of press, expert class, and self-made celebrities, these critics would have to be courted along with those who practiced in the established channels of print and TV. A phenomenon was emerging and the media was trying to put words to it. The *New York Times* mused why bloggers were developing a powerful place in the cosmetics world, saying that, "In many ways, blogs are ideally suited to the pursuit of beauty. The vast number of new products provides plenty of grist for reviews. And because beauty is truly in the eye of the beholder, personal opinion—the *sina qua non* of blogging—matter above all. . . . Where else would you confide to thousands of strangers, 'You are not looking at a pink or red gloss girl. I just don't look good in them. But somehow the tint-gloss combo . . . just shines!'"[11] If harnessed, bloggers could be lightning in a bottle for the beauty industry; women were actively seeking outlets for their fandom, their quest for novelty, and their marketing insights. The age of the makeup influencer was coming, but for the time being, she was still finding her best medium.

Around this time, two seemingly disparate things happened that would shape the conversation around lipstick for more than a decade. In 2007, a then little-known fashion stylist, closet organizer, and celebrity assistant, Kim Kardashian, "leaked" a sex tape, and in 2008, a politician from Alaska, Sarah Palin, kicked off her campaign for the vice presidency by telling folksy jokes about being a working mother. "What's the difference between a hockey mom and a pit bull?" she asked the Republican National Convention in September 2008. The punchline? "Lipstick." The former would cement a new kind of stardom into the popular culture and launch a number of beauty empires; the latter would solidify the link between politics and lipstick for a new era.

Because lipstick has long been saddled with the baggage that comes along with America's expectations of women, it's fair to say that lipstick always has been in some way political. From the modernity of flappers to the morale-building reds of World War II to consumerism against communism of the 1950s and the overt struggles of 1960s feminism, lipstick has managed to find itself a part of the current events conversation. For the twenty-first century, lipstick would appear on both sides of the aisle, as a way of either weaponizing femininity or empowering it. For Palin, beauty was a way of rendering her hard-right beliefs and huge ambitions as benignly folksy and cute. Recognizing good marketing when she saw it, she made the lipstick remark so central to her messaging that a few days later when then-candidate Barack Obama used the cliché "putting lipstick on a pig" in an improvised speech, she was certain it was an attack on her. It may or may not have been, but the Obama campaign still shot back that her offense was a "pathetic attempt to play the gender card."[12] Maryland senator Barbara Mikulski, in turn, countered the whole back-and-forth with "Democratic women, we wear lipstick, too. . . . We don't need another George Bush in earrings going into the number two slot."[13] Which *was* squarely aimed at Palin and at recovering the political football of lipstick wearing. With women voters up for grabs, controlling the narrative as to who best understood womanhood and women's concerns was a big deal; it was a mantle that both teams continue to fight tooth and well-manicured nail.

By the time America was discussing lipsticked pigs, the nation had already seen "stilettos in cow shit,"[14] Fox Studio's nickname for the Paris Hilton reality TV show *The Simple Life*. One of an absolute flood of "reality"-based TV shows, it launched in 2003 to cash in on the public's fascination with Hilton. Born into a wealthy family, she was a puzzling new sort of celebrity. She came from a monied background but acted like more of a *Jersey Shore* "guidette" than a high society Gloria Vanderbilt. Moreover, her fame was meta; she was incredibly famous for being famous, not for any particular skill, avocation, or philanthropy. She was, however, vain, shameless, and thin, which made for great photo ops that captured the public imagination repeatedly for days at a time.

Her public persona could best be described as "sexy baby," a character who came frosted in pink lip gloss and nearly too feminine to function. She was credited with influencing fashion and beauty with her signature color and breathy cooing. "How did this pink proliferation take shape?" asked the papers. "Possibly inspired in part by Paris Hilton, the socialite who is usually seen in a predominantly pink wardrobe."[15] For a while she was the perfect foil for the new era of celebrity endorsement and full-access "reality" entertainment. Also, like Palin, she knocked the hard edges off any ambitions by cloaking them in girlish charms that were seemingly devoid of any intellectual challenge or overt aims. It was sort of genius in its way, and although her moment as America's main topic of conversation ran its course within a few years and flamed out, it set the model for the next "it girl" media and merchandise empires that would come.

The next famous-for-being-famous dynasty actually would come from inside Hilton's own house. Kim Kardashian, the point of entry for the Kardashian-Jenner clan's move into the mainstream, had once worked as a closet organizer and professional friend to Hilton. Like Hilton, she would spin the infamy of a leaked sex tape into a worldwide empire of licensing and multimedia projects, which led to at least half a dozen different cosmetic lines and a somewhat longer-lasting career as a public figure. Kardashian was also born to a wealthy, well-connected family. Her father, Robert Kardashian, had been a high-powered attorney; her stepfather, née Bruce now Caitlyn Jenner, had been an Olympic gold medalist and TV commentator. In a now familiar story arc, Kim was soon quickly, puzzlingly famous for being shapely, taking a great number of pictures, and having her own reality show. Which is not to say that any of this fame was earned, accidental, or organic. No, it was carefully courted and developed by her unstoppable "momager," Kris Jenner, and supported by her large family, who would build their own merchandise empires around it.

Moreover, it was pulled off with the help of an army of stylists, trainers, chefs, doctors, makeup artists, assistants, and hairdressers that kept the family camera ready at all times and on top of every beauty trend—the red lip, the matte lip, the nude lip, the filler-enhanced lip. Whatever it was, someone in the family was on it, which enabled them to become regular, bold names in magazines about how you (as a humble private citizen) could wear the latest look. Kim's smoky eye/neutral lip look was now so signature that it was recommended as a Halloween costume in 2012 along with "sexy zombies" and presidential candidate Mitt Romney. "Makeup artist Renee DiNella said, 'When I think of Kim Kardashian I think of that long black hair and lots of eyeliner and bold lashes with a nude lipstick.'"[16]

This public recognition led to a makeup empire—after some false starts. The same year that Kim was a costume, the Kardashian sisters collectively launched Khroma Beauty. The brand might have caught on with consumers had it not been plagued with legal troubles stemming from the fact that at least two other companies already used some version of the word *chroma*. Khroma Beauty lasted less than a year and was eventually renamed Kardashian Beauty, but even that rebrand didn't help. According to one anonymous source and former employee, the sisters just weren't that into promoting it and it lacked cache. "It was like an accessible drugstore brand,' recalls the source. 'Serious beauty buffs weren't interested in the line, and even though some of the products had cult-like followings, Kardashian Beauty didn't have the industry respect that Kylie Cosmetics and KKW have now.'"[17]

Another issue may have been timing, since it was during this period that influencer culture really broke out in a huge way and celebrity say-so alone was no longer enough to move units. "People are becoming their own experts and they're driving different businesses, like the contour business," said Allure Founding Editor (and then-Editor-in-Chief) Linda Wells at an event celebrating the Best of Beauty Awards. Here was yet another place in American history where lipstick and technology met and fell in love. Within two years of its inception in 2011, *New York Times* described Instagram as a "kind of visual Twitter" and a fashion mecca, which provided manufacturers with "an image bank, a research tool, a showcase for their wares, and now, most compellingly a route into consumers' heads."[18] Additionally a savvy set of content creators was about to change the way brands courted consumers in the biggest way since Hazel Bishop was welcomed into America's living rooms on black-and-white TVs.

The widespread adoption of smartphones, ample platforms begging for content, and endless brand launches came together to create the perfect environment for a new class of taste makers. Additionally, reality TV and the twenty-four-hour news cycle had democratized fame and even what it was to be an expert. Marketers would pinpoint the quality that this generation was looking for as "authenticity," and influencers seemed to have it (or at least could fake it). Some influencers were makeup artists, but some were amateurs in the truest sense: people who just loved makeup and were having fun talking about it. The cagiest among them even managed to figure out a way to monetize their passions and their personalities. The best-loved YouTube and Instagram accounts came to follow a formula: friendly presenters offering their favorite tips, tricks, and products in a light, conversational way. Formerly obscure techniques used for drag and photography, such as contouring and "baking" (i.e., piling a thick layer of powder on top of foundation to set it), entered everyday routines via these tutorials and became the norm until even the *Washington Post* was able to identify the "Instagram look."[19] Which wasn't that hard, since it was usually some obvious variation of an elaborate smoky eye, contoured and highlighted skin, "And finally, it almost always features a matte lip so overdrawn that it can look like an allergic reaction, if not a syringe full of Juvéderm."[20] The inflated mouth was de rigueur, since the vogue for those pneumatic, perpetually pouting lips (whether they were natural, courtesy of prescription fillers, or made via cosmetic magic) was another twenty-first-century, Lolita-type fad that's hard to separate from the rise of the selfie. The trend also would have fallout in subsequent conversations about race and appropriation in makeup, since it would often fetishize on white women, a feature that Black women had long been told to deemphasize in order to meet the racist standards of mainstream beauty.

By 2017, *Forbes* estimated that the top ten beauty influencers had a collective reach of 135,000,000 viewers across YouTube, Instagram, and other social media platforms.[21] For companies wanting to move product, this was an ideal relationship. Some influencers were offered free product in exchange for endorsement, some licensed their names for collections, and some were provided with the capital to back their own signature lines. Launches met with varying degrees of success. Huda Beauty, founded by YouTuber Huda Kattan, is a huge hit with forty million–plus followers on Instagram and is carried in major outlets like Sephora, whereas Jaclyn Hill's lipstick launch was a social media disaster due to failed quality control that resulted in product that was moldy, lumpy, and otherwise unappetizing to fans. Additionally, as with any strategy that's tied to an individual, companies assume the risk of scandal. Makeup artist Jeffree Star, for example, has been plagued by accusations of racism and sexual harassment and was subsequently dropped from his endorsement deal with Morphe cosmetics.

Though influencers are now major players in the beauty space, they aren't the magic bullet between consumers and their cash, and the opinions of industry experts vary on their overall power to influence sales. This has led some venture capitalists and established brands back to the old tried-and-true: celebrities and models. Kylie Jenner, the half-sister of Kim Kardashian, falls somewhere in that spectrum and has managed to spin her Kylie Lip Kits into a huge business (which was quickly expanded and renamed Kylie Beauty). So much hype followed that *Forbes* overshot its praise in 2017 when it laughably described her as "the youngest *self-made* billionaire in the world."[22] Young, yes (she was practically in diapers when Paris Hilton was pioneering the duck-lip selfie); wealthy, totally (sales are huge); self-made, highly debatable. She was born privileged, managed, famous, and with easy access to the capital and connections to infrastructure that makes a big business possible. Which is not exactly the same story as the single-handed stewardship and reputation building that was required of other current beauty entrepreneurs, like the legendary haute couture makeup artist Pat McGrath, when they launched their businesses.

This overvaluation was hardly the only beauty controversy the sisters have been embroiled in. Over the years there have been numerous allegations of cultural appropriation that claim that the sisters thoughtlessly pilfered from Black, Latinx, and Japanese cultures and designers in search of the next big trend. According to the *Daily Beast*, the one upshot that can be found in the Kardashian-Jenner family's problematic behavior is that it has opened an important, if painful, dialogue for consumers about race and recognition in beauty and fashion.

Jenner's tone-deaf cultural appropriation is already grounds for critique. The idea that she literally steals from Black women to turn a profit makes her even more problematic. After all, there's a difference between appropriating a culture and literally snatching somebody's labor. As much as this conversation is bigger than Kylie Jenner and Khloé Kardashian, it's also bigger than these discrete instances, and bigger than an argument over best business practices.[23]

If the Kardashian-Jenners could be said to have a superpower, this was it in a nutshell: they get people talking. For better or worse, they have been given a lot of clout in the current cultural dialogue and their bad behavior may have served to open the door for women of color to have their voices heard on the subject of inclusion in beauty.

In America, women of color seldom have seen themselves represented in beauty in terms of shade selection, models, and brand ownership. The last decade has marked an improvement in inclusion but not a solution. For example, although Beverly Johnson* broke *Vogue*'s color barrier in 1974, more than forty years later, nonwhite cover models were still something of a rarity on the top fashion magazines. According to one 2015 industry report, "Magazine covers are becoming more inclusive, but progress has been startlingly slow. Out of 721 total cover appearances this year (including issues that had multiple covers), 557 of them were white, compared to 164 people of color."[24] Some of that steady improvement can be attributed to the rise of Black women's power in popular culture, sports, and politics. So although Michelle Obama, Serena Williams, and Lupita Nyong'o all have graced the covers of the major magazines, it is often difficult to see that star power integrated into the way the industry handles the needs of women of color. For that reason, women of color increasingly are moving things forward by exercising their own inherent strength as consumers and innovators.

This growth would mark a real change in the way that Black-owned and -centered businesses were viewed in the industry as a whole. No lon-

---

* Not content to rest on her own laurels, Beverly Johnson continues to advocate for measures that would diversify fashion publishing in front of and behind the camera, suggesting in a 2020 *Washington Post* editorial "The Beverly Johnson rule," which "would require at least two black professionals to be meaningfully interviewed for influential positions. This rule would be especially relevant to boards of directors, C-suite executives, top editorial positions and other influential roles."

ger banished to the "ethnic" sections of stores and magazines, these brands were about to flip the script on who made the trends after years of struggle to be financed and recognized. Black-owned or -centered brands have, of course, existed for more than a century but were about to modernize their way of doing business and extend their reach outside the circles they had traditionally served. Fashion Fair, for example, had been founded in 1973 by Eunice Johnson, the wife of *Ebony* magazine publisher, John Johnson, when she couldn't find the right shades of foundation for the models in their fashion shows. The brand was innovative but suffered through the years against newer, trendier competition and the changes the internet brought and, as a result, declared bankruptcy in 2019.

> Fashion Fair faltered. Its original pink compacts and lipstick tubes looked . . . dowdy. The line was refreshed and reintroduced in sleek bronze packaging to great enthusiasm several years ago, but either there wasn't enough product being made or it wasn't being distributed widely. (Explanations vary.) The end result was bare shelves, much to the consternation of worried customers and beauty bloggers.[25]

It was the end of the era for an innovator, but it was also a passing of the torch to a new generation of entrepreneurs and fans.

In particular, Fenty Beauty, the brand launched by singer Rihanna, would drive the trends in a whole new way. A fashion darling and best-selling artist, Rihanna could launch a million imitators. In 2016 *Allure* declared her appearance wearing black lipstick one of the year's most important fashion moments. "Rihanna has always been a walking billboard for badass beauty, so it came as no surprise that at her debut Fenty x Puma runway show in February, she kicked off one of the biggest makeup trends of the year: onyx lips. Now Urban Decay, Kylie Cosmetics, and Maybelline New York all have their own inky lipsticks. But we still consider Rihanna the OG founder of the edgy look."[26] Forty years of goth kids aside, she didn't follow trends, she set them. Given that clout by the press and her fans, it's hard to overstate the importance of her sales power.

She hadn't merely signed her name to a brand that churned out of-the-moment product; by launching a brand that deliberately put women of color first, she was remodeling the way the industry approached customer loyalty. Which was not just right because it was inclusive, it was smart business. According to the *Wall Street Journal,* "After often treating Black women as a marketing afterthought, cosmetics brands are courting these shoppers with blushes, lipsticks, concealers, eyeshadows and foundations designed for them. Such moves come on the heels of the success of Rihanna's beauty line."[27] There were customers of all colors out there and by not acknowledging that, other companies were leaving money on the table. "The multicultural beauty market has been growing faster than the overall market, according to research firm Kline & Company. In 2017, Black consumers in the U.S. spent almost nine times more than non-Blacks on ethnic hair and beauty products, according to a report by Nielsen. During the 52 weeks ending in June 15 of this year, Black women in the U.S. spent $237.8 million on cosmetics, representing 10% of the $2.36 billion spent, Nielsen said."[28] A long-needed shift in representation was finally coming to the entire industry, thanks not just to Rihanna but to a small, but powerful, set of women who were willing to take matters into their own hands.

On the influencer side, women of color were creating tutorials for darker skin tones and trying to highlight brands that had taken their needs into consideration when creating their product.

> The beauty bloggers provide darker-skinned women with something they may not have a tutorial for: the confidence to wear bold colors, to stand up to haters, and, more important, to choose how they present themselves. They try different makeup brands to show that they do work on dark skin or, of course, that they don't. They teach women not to be afraid of color, like red lipstick, bright yellow eye shadow or holographic highlights. Their videos and social media posts are finding an audience of black women who are ready to spend money on beauty products, studies show, but have few choices to pick from.[29]

On the entrepreneur side of the equation, Black-owned indie brands like Mented, Beauty Bakerie, and Lip Bar were generating the influencer and editorial buzz needed to buoy brands in a marketplace that was awash in product launches. In addition, mainstream brands like Too Faced and Lancôme continue to widen the scope of their colors to meet this audience's demands. The result is a move toward marketplace for lipstick that's broader and more driven by the women who consume it than ever before.

Beauty was changing, in part, because America was changing. In the twenty-first century, America was becoming less white, dropping "from 69.1 percent in 2000 to 63.7 percent in 2010"[30] and becoming significantly more Hispanic, Asian, and biracial. While the 45th presidency was desperately clinging to fading influences of our Jim Crow past, a number of citizens were rediscovering the power of grassroots organizing and redefining what it was to be female and powerful in the public space. Congresswoman Alexandria Ocasio-Cortez, in particular, has become a symbol and a lightning rod since her election in the 2018 midterms. The young, outspoken, democratic socialist from New York has already made a deep impact and defied long-held norms and expectations, and developed a huge fanbase in doing so, particularly around the way she has chosen to present herself. Modern, feminine, and bold, her use of lipstick was organically gathering the sort of attention Sarah Palin had been deliberately clamoring for. As *Vanity Fair* noted, "AOC is the perhaps the only member of Congress who moonlights as a beauty influencer: Sharing her go-to red gloss—Stila's Stay All Day Liquid in Beso—translated to a sales spike. 'Every time I go on TV, people ask for my lipstick,' she says. . . . But like Ruth Bader Ginsburg's prickly dissent collar, Ocasio-Cortez's appearance is a study in meaning. The gold hoops and red lips she wore to her first swearing-in were a cosmetic Bat signal to Latina culture and a nod to fellow Bronx native Supreme Court Justice Sonia Sotomayor, who was told not to rock bright nails at her confirmation hearings."[31] For politicians and pundits on the Republican side, her progressive views provided them with all the elements they needed for a new "red scare" and all the attending hyperbole that had followed, but for an increasing segment of the U.S. population, her presence in the media gave them a rare chance to feel seen and celebrated.

Beauty was also becoming inclusive in areas outside of race with the lines around gender expanding slightly. Once again, as America's unofficial ambassador of gender play, RuPaul would be at the forefront of the change. Premiering in 2009, *RuPaul's Drag Race* would make household names of formerly underground performers and help launch a conversation around the limits of gender. Although RuPaul's been pretty clear that he wasn't there for political reasons that doesn't mean it hasn't taken on a life of its own. "Yet for all the cultural fanfare, RuPaul said in a recent interview that 'Drag Race' has never tried to effect change or impart knowledge. 'Our goal is first and foremost to do a show that celebrates drag,' he said. Politics and history are inherent to telling drag artists' stories, often ones of courage and learning how to shine in darkness, he said."[32] It's perhaps for this reason, it was easy for audiences outside the LGBT community to embrace the concept. If there was an agenda there, the reality TV format cloaked it in glamour and gave it a bunch of heartwarming, personal stories, which made it all the more digestible for audiences that might have otherwise rejected it. "Season nine winner and LGBT activist Sasha Velour said it's not fair to expect the show to embody an activist agenda. He called it an introductory course to the art form, not a historical document."[33]

Still, the cheery, almost sports-like tone of the show that encourages viewers to root for their favorites and boo the heels, has allowed performers to build careers and launch brands. Stars Kim Chi, Trixie Mattel, and Miss Fame have all parlayed their success into makeup lines that sell lipstick to women. In addition, several contestants, including Peppermint and Carmen Carrera, have used the platform to raise trans visibility. If not exactly marching in the radical shoes of Marsha P. Johnson, the increased acceptance gave some more mainstream figures the freedom to at least try on what Boy George had cast off. The overall look may be fun, game-show entertainment but the impact on accepting a wider range of gender expressions may prove deeper in the long run.

The new millennium saw lipstick become a new form of entertainment and a symbol of power. No longer merely a part of everyday grooming (although it could be that too), this pocket-sized object could hold the energy of status symbol, tool of self-expression, and agent of social change. Now associated with the powerful and those trying to ascend, it was an empire builder and a way of destroying the status quo. The internet had transformed it and allowed consumers to call the shots about what came next in a way that the industry had never seen before. It could weaponize femininity as a political ploy, as it had been on Sarah Palin, or be a means to empower a younger generation, as it is with Alexandra Ocasio-Cortez. It was a way to fame and money, as it had been for Kylie Jenner, and it was a way to change the game as it had been for Rihanna and Pat McGrath. Its growth and reach were both a part of the blind consumerism that marked the era and a way of making lipstick fulfill the promises of upward mobility, sexual agency, and self-expression that it had whispered to us from advertisements and articles for years.

EPILOGUE
Mask and You Shall Receive

As of this writing, America is in the middle of a once-in-a-century pandemic that has claimed more than half a million lives. Social distancing has cut off millions of us from our usual routine of in-person schooling, work, and socializing. To keep ourselves and others safe, we now wear masks when we leave our homes for even the most mundane activities. The pandemic is frightening, it's unsettling, and it's exposed massive inequities in the way we live and work. It has also, of course, had an impact on lipstick sales and the way we approach beauty in general. Given how central lipstick has become to most women (and some men), will our postpandemic, maskless lives lead to a boost for lip color? Will months and months of going without lead to a glowing future for the industry or show us that we can permanently do without? The casual nature of working from home and the continuing need for masks could be disastrous for a product that's all about conspicuous consumption, or it could drive demand based on craving for a long-denied desire for glamour. It's hard to say with any degree of precision, since there are no exact historical models, but it may be possible to wager an educated guess based on other milestones from our past.

In the global scheme of things, America, not even 250 years old, is a relatively young nation. The closest thing in our history to the current health crisis would be the 1918 influenza pandemic, which killed approximately 675,000 Americans and 50,000,000 people worldwide. When we did emerge from that pandemic (and the concurrent Great War), the

159

nation bounced back in an almost acrobatic fashion. In the popular imagination, the 1920s are almost synonymous with party time. So can we look forward to a new generation of flappers and gin mills? Possibly, although we lack a number of factors that gave the Jazz Age its fizz, namely Prohibition, a "lost generation" of World War I vets, the novelty of votes for women, and a booming economy. That said, Americans have never done well going without, and periods of deprivation (such as the Depression or World War II) are usually followed by wild spending sprees, whereupon consumers indulge themselves in new technologies and the goods that they had been missing during the lean times.

So does that signify that there's a lipstick boom on the horizon? It seems possible given our past behaviors, but we're truly in uncharted territory now with the long-lasting effects of the pandemic and massive shifts in consumer spending habits. During the summer of 2020, luxury brand Shiseido acknowledged the changes and how they impacted its sales. "'Due to COVID-19, consumers' values and behaviors around the world are changing dramatically. . . . [M]akeup [use] like lipstick [is] decreasing as people go out less and wear masks,' Shiseido CEO Masahiko Uotani said on a call with investors last week, after reporting one of the company's worst losses since the early 2000s recession."[1] Which leads to the question of how long this downturn will last. In the absence of any historical information to go on, industry analysts and the beauty press are scrambling to keep busy and make their best guesses. Some have pulled out the old "lipstick index," which they've tried to rebrand as the "skin care index" or the "eye makeup index." Which are logical replacements in a world where everyone is wearing a mask, but it's still built on the fiction of the "lipstick index," so maybe not an ideal way to place one's bets.

The truth is, what we spend our money on currently has changed dramatically and that seismic shift must be factored into any prognostications. So we may have to look outside beauty for a big picture of the way our habits have changed. Take the old, gendered favorite: fancy shoes. Dress shoe sales, high heels in particular, have tanked—dropping 71 percent during the second quarter of 2020,[2] because there's really no reason to wear a power stiletto when you're working from your couch. However, it's not as though people are sitting around barefoot or in bunny slippers. Instead they've shifted from the "work shoe" to something more comfortable and fun, and according to one footwear executive, "with pop colors and prints—the novelty items we had in the product mix," adding that "Customers were shopping less, but what they were looking for when they did buy an item was for it to really bring them joy."[3] This is probably a good model for lipstick. Maybe the high end, the understated, and the elaborate will be off the table for a while due to the economy, our new dress-down look, and the lingering effects of the pandemic, but consumers may find time and money here and there for a classic red satin lipstick or a touch of bright gloss.

Additionally, the future of finding that little bit of joy in a tube again may be tied to emerging technology. More than a century after twist-up tubes were patented, the next big thing in color may be digital. In the spring of 2020, L'Oréal announced that it would launch its Perso device for home use in the first quarter of 2021. This purse-sized dispenser will use artificial intelligence (AI) to make single-use, custom-blended lipsticks in consumers' own homes based on input regarding their wardrobe colors, skin tones, and influencer suggestions. This home technology is still evolving, so the initial offering is only as a liquid lipstick. Other finishes and forms will emerge as the machinery, chemistry, and software are refined and the system becomes less expensive and more widely available. Guive Balooch, head of the company's technology incubator, envisions Perso as freeing consumers to experiment with color without creating clutter, explaining that "With just three cartridges, you can have hundreds of trends and hundreds of recommendations and you can dare to try things without having to have hundreds of products."[4]

Another option in couture lipstick also gaining traction with companies like Finding Ferdinand uses AI online to help customers create their own custom colors. Founder Nhu Le explained that "we are actually already seeing the data and the trends for personalization and customization in terms of customers really dictating the feedback loop for product development."[5] Customers are guided through an interface on Finding Ferdinand's website that helps them blend their own color, select a finish, and choose a scent (or unscented). The company then blends just enough for their order and ships it out, so there's no excess stock or wasted materials. At around $30 a tube, the concept is competitive with most high-end brands and offers the ultimate in exclusivity for those who are willing to start their own trends or looking to replace a discontinued favorite. The other advantage of these technologies is the laser-focused way they produce product, which allows them to continue the important work of inclusivity and sustainability that the industry has begun during the last few years.

In addition to expecting companies to understand them in an "authentic" way, a growing number of consumers is looking at the impact their purchases have on the environment. Beauty is definitely due for some new thought in this area, since it's long been a huge consumer of plastic, global shipping, and compounds from palm oil to petrochemicals, which all have long-term impact on the health of the planet. For these reasons, a number of brands has started to incorporate sustainability measures into their production and distribution plans with varying degrees of sophistication. Some of the newest methods in creating eco-friendly packaging recycle old ideas. Namely, refillable cases, a favorite during World War II, since they saved metal for munitions and kept America beautiful at the same time. Hermès has added luxury to sustainability with its elegant, refillable cases, but since a single color starts at around $67, they're not exactly a solution within reach for most lipstick fans. Fortunately, mass market brands are looking into what they can do to be a part of the conversation, and at least one major player, L'Oréal, has "pledged to make 100 percent of their plastic packaging reusable, refillable, or compostable by 2025."[6] Hopefully this makes some impact, since less than 9 percent of all the plastic packaging that has ever been produced[7] has been recycled; the rest is in our homes, workplaces, clogging up landfills, and polluting the ocean.

Ingredients are another area that brands will have to consider in terms of making products sustainable. Particularly, palm oil, which is used to keep lipstick from melting, is an environmental and labor nightmare. Planting and growing the vast groves of trees necessary to keep up with demand causes deforestation of the natural environment, air pollution, kills orangutangs by destroying their habitat, and has been linked to horrifically exploitive labor practices. A man-made alternative could be a solution and scientists are working on lab-grown substitutes. According to *Huffington Post*, "Experimental alternatives, like oils produced by single-celled organisms such as microalgae or yeasts that are similar to oil palm, are being developed in labs around the world. Lab-grown oils would, at least in theory, take up less land and require far less habitat destruction than traditional crops. But they are still a long way from being economically viable at the scale needed."[8] The flip side of lab-created products is one of optics, since many consumers reject them in the name of the "clean" beauty trend, since "natural" is assumed to be better and healthier. In the meantime, the best solution seems to be purchasing products produced from the more expensive but better monitored oil growers. Moreover, that's just one ingredient out of the many that can go into creating your favorite colors, and as a multibillion-dollar industry, beauty has a lot of issues to tackle if it wants to be a better global citizen and make a positive impact on the climate crisis.

Another promising development during recent years is the drive to make beauty more inclusive at every step. Although the industry is doing better, it still has a long way to go in terms of making sure people of color and along the spectrum of gender see themselves represented in a positive way. These changes must be permanent and systemic, and until that happens there's some justifiable cynicism as to whether diversity is being treated like a hot new trend or whether there's a commitment to necessary long-term work. In the wake of the Black Lives Matter protests of 2020, a number of businesses expressed their support and promised to do better, at least in terms of expanding their line of product shades, if not in executive positions. One artist and activist told the *Pittsburgh Post-Gazette*,

> "Performative activism is what we're seeing right now," says Imani Jahaan, an East Liberty makeup artist, stylist and owner of Imani Jahaan Vintage. "It feels as if George Floyd, Breonna Taylor and Ahmaud Arbery hadn't died, this conversation wouldn't be happening in 2020." She's concerned that "once the hashtags stop trending, things will go back to normal." The change the beauty industry needs "has to be structural," she said.[9]

To wit, only one major retailer, Sephora, has committed to the "15 percent pledge," which "urges retailers to stock as a reflection of the diversity of America's population."[10] Moreover, outside a small—but growing—number of businesses owned by people of color, the boardrooms and product development departments of most corporations remain unchanged. Although the bigger brands have increased their range of shade offerings, entrepreneurs of color, like the women who founded Juvia's Place (African), Ah-Shí Beauty (Native American), and Vive Cosmetics (Latinx) are doing the work to bring colors to market that reflect their looks and culture. Without more representation, things like considering what a "nude" or "neutral" looks like will continue to be centered around a default of white skin. Inclusivity is simply the right thing to do as the population becomes more diverse, and failing to reflect the makeup of its own consumers is a huge miss for the industry.

In addition to the lack of representation of people of color, for a product that is so heavily gendered, the cosmetic industry remains surprisingly male dominated. In 2016 less than 24 percent of executive positions in the beauty business of established companies were held by females (start-ups fared way better at 53 percent),[11] which means that decisions about what women want and how to give it to them can conceivably be made without women being involved. Plus, although gender rules are slightly less rigid, there's been no real push to sell lipstick to cis het men. Any movement toward selling cosmetics to men has largely been as an extension of skin care (e.g., moisturizers that contain a skin-colored tint) and are met with skepticism; color cosmetics remain a step too far even for the most fashion-forward, straight American males. Perhaps this will shift as trends and attitudes change, but in the short term, visible makeup for men is still a very hard sell.

For gay and gender nonconforming individuals, again, things are better but still evolving in terms of representation. This is another area where newer brands are leading the way—and trying to do so in a manner that avoids tokenizing or exploiting gender difference. For example, Fluide, which describes itself as "a mission-driven beauty brand that creates vegan, cruelty-free and paraben-free cosmetics designed for all skin shades and gender expressions," wants to see more than the occasional gender nonconforming and/or BIPOC model. As company cofounder Isabella Giancarlo explained its vision to *Fast Company*, "I would like to see more queer people being represented not just in the campaigns that these brands are featuring, but behind the lens as well—as art directors, in management positions—because that would make those efforts come across as more genuine and authentic."[12] As with racial diversity, this is an area in which having the right people in on the conversation ultimately determines how (and if) the industry moves forward.

More established players are not standing idly by in the face of these changes. In addition to having a number of models representing people of color and a range of gender expressions, MAC changed one of its signature taglines due to employee feedback. "According to Nancy Mahon, who heads up the MAC AIDS Fund (a nonprofit arm set up in 1994), a single staffer spoke up at a town hall. 'I don't understand why our tagline is 'all sexes.' It really should be 'all genders,'' she recalls the employee saying. A few months later, MAC made the change. Its new tagline reads: 'All Ages, All Races, All Genders.'" Which, again, is a positive step, but one that MAC and others in the lipstick business must follow with sincere and profound change or run the risk of being perceived as patronizing and exploitive. As nonbinary writer Riley R. L., put it in *Teen Vogue*,

> If we place our trust in advertising to advance our cause rather than sharing our stories on our own terms, we're passing them over to those whose primary goal is to profit from them. These sanitized, corporate narratives run the risk of leading young queer people to believe that embodying their identity is as simple as buying the right lipstick or wearing the right nail polish, instead of expressing themselves in whatever way feels true to them.[13]

This is a real and valid concern in an industry whose legacy of empowerment and self-expression is so incredibly intertwined with its need for sales and for creating demand through insecurity. As lipstick advances and expands to include more people in the definition of what it is to be beautiful, our relationships with lipstick must remain complex and mindful.

~

This is the way of all of our history. When trying to make sense of America and its legacy of racism, James Baldwin wrote, "History is not the past. It is the present. We carry our history with us. We are our history." The same holds true for lipstick. Lipstick can be a small joy, but it's also one that holds the weight of the sins of our shared past. It's a lens for viewing how far we've come and how far we still have to go. It embodies the heritage of the way we talk to women about their value and their wants; the priorities and the boundaries we give to race, class, and gender, and the power of purchase. It's viewed as frivolous and yet it's no small thing. It's been to war, to space, and in the halls of power. In the hands of Marsha P. Johnson, Alexandra Ocasio-Cortez, and others, it's drawn the battle lines in the fight for equity from the most marginalized among us. It's built empires for women from Helena Rubinstein to Pat McGrath and given the establishment the middle finger on Iggy Pop and Debbie Harry. We've both rejected it and embraced it in the name of feminism. It's both part of the language and a visual shorthand for sex and sexuality. Through the years, we have imbued this little object with our big dreams of beauty, visibility, and upward mobility. This is its history. Its future is as unwritten as any other, but its past holds our story.

ACKNOWLEDGMENTS

There are a lot of people who teach you to wear lipstick and generally just push you forward in your endeavors, so here's to them:

First and foremost, there is my mother, Thelma H. Carter, PhD, who would end my teenage crying jags by instructing me, "Go wash your face and put on lipstick. You'll feel better." My mensch of a brother, Adam C. Carter, MD, and his family, Margot, Jack, and Exy. Susan and Eli Gilbert and Elaine Zimbler, for being our support system in this difficult year. *Beaucoup des mes cousines Français, aussi.*

To my chosen family of friends, who gave you reason to wear it out of the house: Meirav Devash, Christine Colby, Emma Allen (and the ladies of Fuckin' Ladies Brunch), Eddie McNamara, Mitch Adair, Marijana Sprajc, Joli Beauchamp, A. V. Phibes, Josh Nahas (the original Red Menace), Robb Teer, Corinne Butler, Rachel Guidera (Rock in Peace), Lucirene Pina, Katy Mastorokis, Sunny Buick, and Cori Werner (along with her glamorous mom, Maribeth, may her memory be a blessing.)

As a performer, there are those who helped me give life to my inner drag queen: Flawless Mother Sabrina ("If you don't think you're the most interesting person in the room, no one is going to do it for you"), World Famous *Bob*, who understands what it is to be a "female-female impersonator," and those who pushed the "working act": Jo Weldon, James Taylor, Alex Doll, Tigger!, Fem Appeal, and Elayne Boosler.

ACKNOWLEDGMENTS

As a writer, William Ferguson, Tim Travaligni, Jake Bonar, Julie Tibbott, Doreen Bloch and the staff of the Makeup Museum, John Strausbaugh, Tonya Hurley, and the education department at Elizabeth Arden.

And those who aren't here with us now but would love to have seen it: Helen Zias, Sam Alford, my beloved uncle Dan Hyman, PhD, my zaide Jack, and my bubbe Rose Hyman (who never actually owned a lipstick herself), my "Aunt" Aimee Mast, who always (may her memory be a blessing) had lipstick on her teeth, Mimi Szafran, and my "Aunt" Bella Shore.

And again, thanks to my dad and biggest fan, Maurice C. Carter, MD.

NOTES

Chapter One: Red Coats of Another Sort

1. Elizabeth Arden Inc., "March on in Our Founder's Footsteps," www.elizabetharden.com/march-on.html.

2. Advertisement, *Pennsylvania Gazette*, August 28, 1766, 1.

3. Advertisement, *Pennsylvania Gazette*, August 28, 1766, 1.

4. *Records of the Governor and Company of the Massachusetts Bay in New England* (Boston: Printed by order of the legislature, 1853), 126.

5. *Martha Washington's recipe for "the finest lip salve in the world," copied out by Eleanor Parke Custis, adopted daughter of the Washingtons, for Natalie, Mathilde, Clementine, Oscar, and Edmond Lafayette*, December 17, 1824, Cornell University, Collection 4661, Box 3, Folder 39.

6. Rev. John Bennett, *Letters to a Young Lady on a Variety of Useful and Interesting Subjects: Calculated to Inform the Heart, to Form the Manners, and Enlighten the Understanding* (Philadelphia: W. Spotswood and H. and P. Rice, 1793), 107.

7. John Prentiss, *The Compleat Toilet, or Ladies' Companion: A Collection of the Most Approved and Simple Methods of Preparing Baths, Essences, Pomatums, Powders, Perfumes, and Sweet-Scented Waters* (New York: Mott and Hunter, 1794), 40.

8. Letter from Abigail Adams to John Adams, 31 March–5 April 1776, Adams Family Papers: An Electronic Archive, Massachusetts Historical Society, www.masshist.org/digitaladams.

9. Judith Sargent Murray, "On the Equality of the Sexes," in *Early American Writing*, ed. Giles Gunn (New York: Penguin Books, 1994), 550.

10. "Vendors of Cosmetics Rebuked," *Graham Journal of Health and Longevity*, November 23, 1839, 3.

11. "The Effects of Cosmetics on the Skin," *American Agriculturist* (1842–1850), January 1848, 7.

12. Barnabus Breef, "Doctor Moral's: Celebrated Attracting Lip Salve," *The Port-Folio* (1801–1827), April 30, 1803, 3.

13. "Approved Cosmetic," *Guardian and Monitor: A Monthly Publication Devoted to the Moral Improvement of the Rising Generation* (1825–1828), December 1, 1826, 407.

14. "Approved Cosmetic," *Guardian and Monitor*, 407.

15. "The Season," *Connecticut Courant* (1791–1837), December 8, 1818, 1.

16. "The Belle," *Olive Branch* (Boston), February 14, 1852, 2.

17. "On Artificial Coloring," *Graham's American Monthly Magazine of Literature, Art & Fashion*, July 1, 1855, 91.

18. "The City Belle," *Lantern* (New York), December 25, 1852, 267.

19. "Festoon of Fashion," *Port-Folio* (1801–1827), January 21, 1802, 2.

20. "Editor's Table," *The Lady's Book*, October 1, 1836, 189.

21. "True Americanism," *Louisville Morning Courier and American Democrat* (1844–1846), December 4, 1844, 2.

22. "Cosmetics—Their Use and Manufacture," *Scientific American*, March 8, 1862, 151.

Chapter Two: The Rouge Badge of Courage

1. "The Last Fashion," *Saturday Evening Post* (1839–1885), May 17, 1862, 2.

2. "The Lady in Black," *Boston Herald* (1846–1865), June 14, 1862, 1.

3. "A Fearful Record of Murders-Vigilance Committees at Work," *San Francisco Examiner*, May 18, 1867, 5.

4. "Fashion Lecture by Montes Last Evening," *Cincinnati Daily Enquirer* (1852–1872), February 21, 1860, 2.

5. "General Health and Disease: Injurious Effects of Cosmetics," *Christian Advocate* (1866–1905), February 6, 1868, 47.

6. J. Scoffern, "Beautiful for Ever," *Eclectic Magazine of Foreign Literature* (1844–1898), September 1868, 8.

7. Scoffern, "Beautiful for Ever," 8.

8. "The Fashionable Woman," *Albion: A Journal of News, Politics and Literature* (1822–1876), August 29, 1868, 46.

9. "Map of Predominating Sex Showing the Local Excess of Males or of Females in the Distribution of Population over the Territory of the United States East of the 100th Meridian. Compiled from the Statistics of Population at the Ninth Census 1870. By Francis A. Walker. (Julius Bien, Lith., 1874)."

10. "Beautifying the Eyes," *Daily Nebraska State Journal*, September 23, 1889, 5.

11. "Making Old Women Young," *Chickasaw County Times*, February 2, 1876, 6.

12. "Poisonous Face Powders," *Garfield Banner*, October 15, 1881, 11.

13. "The Vice of Painting," *San Francisco Chronicle*, November 18, 1883, 4.

14. "Physiology: The Secret of Beauty," *American Phrenological Journal* (1838–1869), January 1864, 8.

15. "Physiology: The Secret of Beauty," 8.

16. "Our Young Girls," *Baltimore Sun*, January 1, 1870, 4.

17. U.S. Census Bureau, 1880 Census of Population and Housing.

18. "In Lillian Russell's Place," *New York Times*, May 13, 1885, 8.

19. "Business Points: A Strange Coincidence," *Detroit Free Press*, September 25, 1885, 5.

20. Advertisement, *New York Herald*, March 11, 1883, 22.

21. Advertisement, *Riverside Daily Press*, January 12, 1893, 2.

22. Advertisement, *News and Courier—Sunday News*, February 22, 1881, 2.

23. "Toilet Mysteries: Some of the Requisits [*sic*] Which Go to Make up a Really Charming Society Girl," *Chicago Daily Tribune*, July 6, 1884, 13.

24. "For Women Readers," *Philadelphia Inquirer*, May 18, 1890, 4.

25. "Woman's World and Work," *Times-Picayune* (published as the *Daily Picayune*), May 14, 1893, 24.

26. "How Women Bathe in Paris," *Hall's Journal of Health* 39, no. 5 (1892): 112.

27. "Young Men Who Use Cosmetics," *Cincinnati Enquirer*, September 30, 1883, 9.

28. "Cosmetics for Men: Cincinnati Gentlemen Who Visit the Beautifying Artist," *Cincinnati Enquirer*, September 27, 1885, 13.

29. "Exposing the Men: A Drug Clerk Tells What He Thinks He Knows," *Boston Daily Globe*, August 24, 1885, 5.

30. "Modern Complexions," *Harper's Bazaar*, September 6, 1884, 561–62.

31. Arthur Stanley, "Touching the Toilet," *Good Housekeeping*, October 1892, 167–69.

32. Marquise de Panhael, "Beauty: How to Be Beautiful: Chapter X, Maquillage," *Vogue*, December 6, 1894, 370.

33. "Seen in the Shops," *Vogue*, October 11, 1900, 236.

Chapter Three: Speak Softly and Carry a Lip Stick

1. "Age Restored to Youth," *Philadelphia Inquirer*, February 3, 1901, 4.

2. "Alexandra's Approval of Rouge," *Kansas City Star*, July 3, 1904, 12.

3. "Alexandra's Approval of Rouge."

4. U.S. Census Bureau, "20th Century Statistics," *Statistical Abstract of the United States: 1999* (December 1999): 868.

5. U.S. Census Bureau, "20th Century Statistics."

6. U.S. Census Bureau, "20th Century Statistics."

7. U.S. Census Bureau, "20th Century Statistics," 879.

8. "Lip Salve Always with Her," *Boston Daily Globe*, December 16, 1900, 37.

9. Advertisement, *Pittsburgh Press*, May 19, 1910, 7.

10. Federal Highway Administration, "Motor Vehicle Registrations, by States, 1900–1995," n.d., https://www.fhwa.dot.gov/ohim/summary95/mv201.pdf, 1.

11. "Frills of Fashion," *Charleston News and Courier* (published as the *Sunday News*), February 3, 1907, 22.

12. "Teaching Women Art of Make-Up," *San Francisco Chronicle*, July 1, 1906, 6.

13. Advertisement, *Boston Herald*, April 10, 1900, 9.

14. Advertisement, *Omaha Illustrated Bee*, February 25, 1906, 6.

15. Advertisement, *Boston Herald*, April 10, 1900, 9.

16. "Making over the Suffragette," *Chicago Daily Tribune*, April 25, 1909, F6.

17. "Making over the Suffragette."

18. Maggie Whiteman Steward, "Cosmetic and Hair Straighteners," *Star of Zion*, March 21, 1901, 5.

19. Marie Vantini, "How to Use Rouge and Powder," *Baltimore Sun*, May 16, 1909, 18.

20. "Use of Cosmetics Overdone," *Daily Home News*, October 9, 1913, 14.

21. Nixola Greeley-Smith, "Too Much Paint on New York Women's Cheeks," *Pittsburgh Press*, November 11, 1912, 10.

22. Ida McGlone-Gibson, "Using Rouge Is Not a Matter of Morality, One of Taste," *Pittsburgh Press*, August 18, 1914, 10.

23. "Beauty: The Old Order Passes," *Vogue*, October 1, 1913, 94.

24. "Milady's Friend: Her Dressing Table," *Photoplay*, July–December 1916, 161.

25. Alice Joyce, "How to Make-Up," *Picture-Play*, September 1917–February 1918, 238.

26. "Screen Gossip," *Picture-Play*, March–August 1917, 270.

27. Epes Winthrop-Sargeant, "Advertising for Exhibitors," *Moving Picture World*, March 9, 1918, 1272.

28. "Substitutes Stamp Tax for Gross Sales Plan," *(Washington, DC) Evening Star*, May 28, 1917, 1.

29. "Senate Strikes out Proposals in the Revenue Bill," *Winston-Salem Journal*, May 27, 1917, 1.

30. "Substitutes Stamp Tax for Gross Sales Plan"; "Senate Strikes out Proposals in the Revenue Bill."

31. Barbara Craydon, "Lip Stick, and Powder Puff Discarded Now for Paint Brush," *Louisville Courier-Journal*, July 28, 1918, C8.

32. "Women Factor in Winning War," *Aberdeen Daily News*, June 14, 1918, 1.

33. "Luxuries Must Go Say Women," *Wichita Daily Eagle*, April 16, 1917, 2.

34. "Luxury and Necessities in the Same Molecule," *Women's Wear Daily*, May 24, 1918, 1.

Chapter Four: The Glossed Generation

1. "Defies School Board Anti-Cosmetic Rule," *Miami News*, December 21, 1921, 21.

2. "$1,000 a Week, Miss Pugsley Is Offered," *Arkansas Democrat*, December 14, 1921, 6.

3. "Noted Lipstick Case Coming Up Soon," *Evening Tribune*, December 25, 1921.

4. Pugsley v. Sellmeyer, 158 Ark. 247, Arkansas Supreme Court (1923).

5. "Beauty and Votes," *Arkansas Democrat*, September 16, 1920, 6.

6. "Beauty in Politics," *Lansing State Journal*, August 28, 1920, 4.

7. "The Lipstick War," *Miami District Daily News*, July 8, 1920, 4.

8. "The Lipstick War," 4.

9. "Tremendous Enthusiasm Is Report from W.C.T.U.," *Tucson Citizen*, August 22, 1921, 4.

10. "WCTU Declines to Wage 'Lip-Stick War' in Baltimore," *Baltimore Sun*, July 1, 1920, 8.

11. "'Godless Gayety' Scores McCaul," *Brooklyn Daily Times*, April 30, 923, 7.

12. "'Girls as Moral as Ever,' a New York Pastor," *Kansas City Star*, April 21, 1922, 13.

13. Frederic J. Haskin, "In Defence of Flappers," *San Diego Union*, April 9, 1921, 4.

14. "Great Sum Is Invested in America for Taxable Luxuries," *Cincinnati Enquirer*, October 16, 1920, 1.

15. U.S. Census Bureau, "20th Century Statistics," *Statistical Abstract of the United States: 1999* (December 1999): 869.

16. "How Poor We Are!" *Davenport Democrat and Leader*, October 19, 1920, 6.

17. "Eats Her Height in Lipstick Every Four Years," *Des Moines Register*, June 14, 1925, 45.

18. "Fifty Million Painted Lips Kissed Everyday!—And No One Gets Poisoned," *Indianapolis Star*, September 7, 1924, 77.

19. U.S. Census Bureau, "20th Century Statistics," 868.

20. Advertisement, *Camera!* April 1922, 17.

21. Max Factor, "Movie Makeup," *American Cinematographer*, April 1928, 8.

22. Advertisement, *Kansas City Times*, August 17, 1925, 9.

23. Edward T. Folliard, "Sheen of the Silver Screen," *Washington Post*, April 19, 1925, SO13.

24. "Queens Bow to Hollywood's Master of Makeup," *Sunday Star*, March 10, 1929, 89.

25. Advertisement, *Evening Star*, January 19, 1926, 12.

26. Advertisement, *Evening Star*, January 19, 1926, 12.

27. Advertisement, *Screenland*, April 1929, 89.

28. "Two Women Flyers to Try Flights to Europe," *Boston Globe*, August 22, 1927, 13.

29. "Ruth Elder Hops Off Today," *Daily News*, October 1, 1927, 3.

30. "Flapper Wings for Paris," *Daily News*, October 12, 1927, 3.

31. "Message from Woman Flyer," *Boston Globe*, October 13, 1927, 1.

32. "Captain of Steamer Tells about Rescue of Fliers at Sea," *Alexandria Daily Town Talk*, October 15, 1927, 1.

Chapter Five: In the Red

1. "The Gospels of Beauty," *Vogue*, February 15, 1932, 64, 65, 88.

2. "Yearly Beauty Bill Put at $750,000,000," *New York Times*, October 1, 1930, 28.

3. Sarah E. Hill, Christopher D. Rodeheffer, Vladas Griskevicius, Kristina Durante, and Andrew Edward White, "Boosting Beauty in an Economic Decline: Mating, Spending, and the Lipstick Effect," *Journal of Personality and Social Psychology* 103, no. 2 (2012): 275–91, https://doi.org/10.1037/a0028657.

4. Antoinette Donnelly, "Lives There a Woman Who Is Happy without Lipstick?" *Chicago Daily Tribune* (1923–1963), March 7, 1938, 19.

5. Ruth B. Savord, "Work Opportunities in American Fashion Design," Proceedings of the Conference Held in New York City, April 23–24, 1941.

6. U.S. Bureau of Labor Statistics, "Labor Force, Employment, and Unemployment, 1929–39: Estimating Methods," www.bls.gov/opub/mlr/1948/article/pdf/labor-force-employment-and-unemployment-1929-39-estimating-methods.pdf.

7. Antoinette Donnelly, "Experts Will Make Plain Jane a Beauty: Pledge Daily Miracle at World's Fair," *Chicago Daily Tribune* (1923–1963), August 5, 1933, 11.

8. "Beauty Is Part of Your Job," *Good Housekeeping*, October 1936, 37.

9. Hope Ridings Miller, "Mrs. Roosevelt Adopts Lipstick, Hint of Rouge," *Washington Post*, February 15, 1938, 1.

10. Blanche Wiesen Cook, *Eleanor Roosevelt*, vol. 3: *The War Years and After* (New York: Penguin, 2017), 21.

11. "Posse Ambush Slays Bandit and Gun Girl," *Pittsburgh Post-Gazette*, May 24, 1934, 4.

12. "Working Women in the 1930s," in *American Decades*, vol. 4, *1930–1939*, ed. Judith S. Baughman, Victor Tomkins, Victor Bondi, and Tandy McConnell (Detroit, MI: Gale, 2001).

13. "Scab Stripped Naked," *Daily Worker*, September 5, 1935, 2.

14. "Scab Stripped Naked," 2.

15. "$750,000,000: Women of America Are Not Cutting Down on Cosmetics, Manufacturers Are Told," *New York Times*, October 1, 1930, P28.

16. Advertisement, *Ladies' Home Journal*, October 1937, 122.

17. Advertisement, *Ladies' Home Journal*, March 1936, 133.

18. Advertisement, *Ladies' Home Journal*, August 1931, 36.

19. Grace Mack, "Right about Face," *Ladies' Home Journal*, March 1934, 29.

20. "Getting along with Your Own Face," *Good Housekeeping*, February 1937, 90, 91, 219.

21. "Wallflower into Orchid," *Good Housekeeping*, December 1933, 54–55.

22. "Beauty: A Course in Painting Offered by *Vogue*," *Vogue*, November 15, 1931, 64, 64, 65, 126.

23. "Extension Course in College Beauty," *Vogue*, August 15, 1938, 146, 147.

24. Ann Boyd, "Making Up in Hollywood: Helen Twelvetrees Tells You about What Every Movie Star Knows about Judicious Use of Makeup," *New Movie Magazine*, December 1933, 62.

25. Sydney Valentine, "Miracles of Makeup," *New Movie Magazine*, October 1930, 18–19.

26. "How to Look Your Best: Make-Up Hints," *New York Amsterdam News* (1922–1938), December 3, 1930, 6.

27. Emmita Cardozo, "Paris Beauty Expert Writes for Women: The Pursuit of Beauty," *New York Amsterdam News* (1922–1938), July 17, 1937, 9.

28. Vivian Morris, "Harlem Beauty Shops," Folklore Project, Life Histories, 1936–39, U.S. Work Projects Administration, Federal Writers' Project.

29. "Scientific Unit to Weigh 'Ads' for Cosmetics: New Board of Standards," *New York Herald Tribune*, December 3, 1936, 43.

30. "Teeth of Law to Clamp Down upon Poisonous Lipsticks," *Washington Post*, June 22, 1939, 1.

31. "Effect of Law in Cosmetics Selling Noted," *Women's Wear Daily*, January 17, 1939, 14, 39.

32. C. P. Thompson, "Billion-Dollar Whims," *New York Herald Tribune*, January 19, 1936, 1.

33. "Nazi Lambasts Jews, Czechs, and Lipsticks," *Chicago Daily Tribune*, June 27, 1938, 2.

34. "Nazi Elite Guard Calls Cosmetics a 'Humbug,'" *New York Herald Tribune* (1926–1962), June 1, 1939, 4.

35. "What! No Purple?" *Washington Post*, October 29, 1940, 4.

36. "Gas-Repellent Suit of Oil Silk Featured by London Store," *Women's Wear Daily*, September 14, 1939, 1.

37. "Style Show Theme Is Latin America," *New York Times*, June 27, 1940, 28.

Chapter Six: Beauty Is Your Duty

1. Carolyn Abbott, "War Promotes Cosmetics' Use, Say Beauticians," *Washington Post*, October 8, 1941, 17.

2. J. C. Furnas, "Glamour Goes to War," *Saturday Evening Post*, November 29, 1941, 19.

3. "Lipsticks, Nail Polish, Rouge, Curtailed by New WPB Order," *Baltimore Sun*, July 17, 1942, 1.

4. Kathryn Barnwell, "Lipstick Containers Can Fight the Japs," *Atlanta Constitution*, November 1, 1942, 2D.

5. Advertisement, *Cosmopolitan*, November 1942, 145.

6. Ted Gill, "Scrap Rubber Pile Gets Kissing Machine Lips," *Baltimore Sun*, August 9, 1942, SM4.

7. Lydia Lane, "Feminine Role in National Defense Starts at Beauty Shop, Says Expert," *Los Angeles Times*, February 18, 1942, B16.

8. "Italy Aids Women to Keep Looks while Nazis Impose Dowdiness," *New York Times*, June 3, 1942, 19.

9. Anne O'Hare, "Homemaking under Hitler," *Ladies' Home Journal*, October 1933, 10.

10. Erika Thomas, *Max Factor and Hollywood: A Glamorous History* (Charleston, SC: History Press, 2016), 89.

11. Tania Long, "Cosmetics Benefit Morale in Britain," *New York Times*, April 28, 1942, 18.

12. "Cosmetics Go to Britain Too," *New York Times*, November 11, 1941, 28.

13. Lula Garrett, "Lipstick," *Baltimore Afro-American* (1893–1988), September 5, 1942, 4.

14. Patricia Lindsay, "Women Taught Beauty Guards for War Jobs," *Baltimore Sun*, November 1, 1942, SM8.

15. "Lipstick Kiss Banned," *Washington Post*, August 23, 1944, 2.

16. "Bags for Pistols and Lipsticks Given to City's Policewomen: Combining Business with Beauty," *New York Herald Tribune*, September 25, 1943, 1.

17. "Practical Fashion for Lady Conductors," *New York Times*, July 4, 1944, 16.

18. "Director Named and Feminine 'West Point' Okayed as Roosevelt Signs Bill Authorizing 150,000 Force," *Baltimore Sun*, May 16, 1942, 2.

19. Ruth Cowan, "Director Hobby of the WAAC Okays Lipstick," *Atlanta Constitution*, May 17, 1942, 8A.

20. Carolyn Abbot, "War Necessitates New Beauty Regime," *Washington Post*, January 3, 1942, 13.

21. Lieutenant Bess Stephenson, "WACs Want Dainties for Christmas Gifts," *Washington Post*, November 7, 1943, L5.

22. Patricia Bronte, "Lipstick Corps Shows Ability Herding Jeeps: Red Cross Unit Puts Cars through Paces at McPherson," *Constitution*, June 21, 1942, 2B.

23. "Women Aim Rifles Handily as Lipstick," *New York Times*, January 14, 1942, 19.

24. Martha Parker, "Lipsticks Better Than in Long Time," *New York Times*, June 16, 1944, 16.

25. "New Lipstick Cases to Be Made Lighter," *New York Times*, August 12, 1944, 8.

26. Barbara Heggie, "People and Ideas: Back on the Pedestal, Ladies," *Vogue*, January 15, 1946, 78, 118.

27. "Thousands of British Brides Given Tips on American Habits," *Atlanta Constitution*, January 1, 1945, 1.

28. Jean Kinkead, "America's Faces," *Cosmopolitan*, March 1945, 21.

Chapter Seven: The Red Menace

1. "A Little Lipstick, a Lot of Brains," *(Ridgewood, NJ) Sunday News*, February 29, 1948, 18.

2. "GOP View Dim on Lipstick Aid," *Pittsburgh Press*, May 1, 1948, 2.

3. "Nylons and Lipstick Ruin Marshall Plan Says a Greek," *Lathrop (MO) Optimist*, February 23, 1950, 7.

4. J. A. Livingstone, "Business Outlook," *(New Brunswick, NJ) Sunday Times*, April 18, 1948, 6.

5. Beth Harber, "Learn How," *Seventeen*, January 1951, 56–57.

6. "How Old Is Old Enough," *Seventeen*, April 1951, 4.

7. Patricia Fair, "Good Looks for the Young Beauty in Your House," *Parents'*, September 1950, 102.

8. Lucile D. Kirk, "Toiletries Made Especially for Little Girls," *Good Housekeeping*, February 1955, 108.

9. Advertisement, *Parents' Magazine & Family Home Guide*, February 1955, 108.

10. Gisela Kahn Gresser, "I Went to Moscow," *Ladies' Home Journal*, October 1950, 48.

11. Laura Lou Bookman and Peter Briggs, "They Let Us Talk to the Russians," *Ladies' Home Journal*, June 1955, 50, 149.

12. Bookman and Briggs, "They Let Us Talk to the Russians," 151.

13. "'Tattle-Tale Red' on Way Out Smear-Proof Lipstick Making Firm Hold in Cosmetics Industry," *Madera Daily News-Tribune*, September 4, 1951, 3.

14. "Woman Chemist Hits Jackpot," *Business Week*, 1951, 48.

15. "Stockholder Suit of Hazel Bishop Goes to Trial," *Women's Wear Daily*, February 12, 1954, 8.

16. "Quiz Show Is Big Gun in Lipstick War," *Ventura County Star-Free*, October 15, 1959, 34.

17. "New Investing Group Acquires Stock Control of Hazel Bishop," *New York Times*, December 15, 1959, 59.

18. "Former Cafe Bouncer in Orient President of Hazel Bishop, Inc.," *New York Times*, March 31, 1960, 51.

19. "Boards of Lanolin Plus and Hazel Bishop Agree in Principle to Merge," *Wall Street Journal*, August 28, 1961, 20.

20. "She's No Jane Russell, Says Male Reporter," *Fort Worth Star-Telegram*, February 13, 1953, 4.

21. "To a Woman, Chris Belongs to the Tribe," *Fort Worth Star-Telegram*, February 13, 1953, 4.

22. "Christine Back in the U.S.: She Left as G.I. George and Is Very Girlish," *Cincinnati Enquirer*, February 13, 1953, 3.

23. "Christine Steps Out," *(Chambersburg, PA) Public Opinion*, December 31, 1952, 8.

24. Advertisement, *Jet*, June 2, 1955, 67.

25. Advertisement, *Ebony*, November 1959, 97.

Chapter Eight: The Cosmetic Counterculture

1. "Does Jackie Have a Glove Secret?" *Cleveland Call and Post*, April 7, 1962, 5B.

2. "Teen-Age Report to the Nation: No More Jive—It's out of Orbit," *Ladies' Home Journal*, January 1960, 43.

3. Peter Bart, "Advertising: Teen-Age Markets Are Wooed," *New York Times*, September 8, 1963, F14.

4. Bart, "Advertising," F14.

5. "Shaping the '60's . . . Foreshadowing the '70's," *Ladies' Home Journal*, January 1962, 79, 30.

6. "Shaping the '60's," 79, 30.

7. Charles Revson, "What I Don't Know about Women," *Cosmopolitan*, June 1960, 62–67.

8. Advertisement, *Vogue*, October 1, 1960, 20, 21.

9. Advertisement, *Seventeen*, July 1962, 6–7.

10. Advertisement, *Ladies' Home Journal*, October 1967, 23.

11. Advertisement, *Vogue*, February 1, 1968, 44, 45.

12. Advertisement, *Seventeen*, September 1969, 7.

13. Jane Wilson, "The Compleat (Hippie) Girl," *Cosmopolitan*, January 1968, 62–67, 109.

14. Art Buchwald, "Braless Babes?" *Rockland County Journal-News*, September 12, 1968.

15. Charlotte Curtis, "Miss America Pageant Is Picketed by 100 Women," *New York Times*, September 8, 1968, 81.

16. "Face to Face with Miss Black America," *Seventeen*, March 1969, 151.

17. George F. Brown, "The 'Untouched Style' Still Going Strong in New York," *Pittsburgh Courier*, August 4, 1962, 6.

18. Cathy Aldridge, "Bye, Bye Purple Lipstick, and Nut Brown Powder!" *New York Amsterdam News*, May 17, 1969, 5.

19. "Black Is Beautiful: Cosmetics for Negro Women," *(Zanesville, OH) Times Recorder*, October 12, 1969, 26.

20. Rosalyn Abrevaya, "Beauty Goes Psychedelic!" *Family Weekly*, September 10, 1967, 9.

21. "Fashion Reaction," *Women's Wear Daily*, June 12, 1968, 4–5.

Chapter Nine: Never Mind the Lipsticks

1. Steve Watson, "Stonewall 1979: The Drag of Politics," *Village Voice*, June 15, 1979, www.villagevoice.com/2019/06/04/stonewall-1979-the-drag-of-politics/.

2. "The 'Gay' People Demand Their Rights," *New York Times*, July 5, 1970, 100.

3. Arthur Evans, "Should TVs Embarrass Gay Cause?" *Advocate*, May 23, 1973, 37.

4. Steve Watson, "Stonewall 1979: The Drag of Politics," *Village Voice*, June 15, 1979, www.villagevoice.com/2019/06/04/stonewall-1979-the-drag-of -politics/.

5. Nathan Cobb, "Dolls, Masc. & Fem.," *Boston Globe*, February 10, 1974, A34.

6. Nathan Cobb, "Lou Reed and The Glitter Thing," *Boston Globe*, February 18, 1973, B12.

7. Bruce Meyer, "Dolls Coarse, Popular," *Atlanta Constitution*, September 21, 1973, 6C.

8. Advertisement, *Boston Globe*, March 9, 1975, A4.

9. Sara Davidson, "Makeup without Guilt," *Cosmopolitan*, November 1977, 162, 164, 166, 186–87.

10. Jill Robinson, "Pretty: What It Means," *Vogue*, January 1, 1976, 63, 65, 66, 69.

11. "Women's Movement Boosts Cosmetics, Maker Says," *Philadelphia Inquirer*, May 9, 1974, 12C.

12. Marian Christy, "Cosmetic Industry Undergoes Facelift," *Boston Globe*, September 29, 1972, 32.

13. Marian Christy, "Charles Revson: A Pox on Women's Lib," *Boston Globe*, February 6, 1972, A15.

14. Marian Christy, "Cosmetics Giants Advocate Pooling Feminism, Femininity," *Austin American Statesman*, November 28, 1979, C6.

15. Advertisement, *Cosmopolitan*, March 1979, 127.

16. George F. Will, "What a Year," *Newsweek*, December 26, 1977, 10.

17. Otis James, "Dolly's Figure Isn't Her Only Outstanding Feature," *Lexington Herald*, November 19, 1978, 73.

18. Robin Adams Sloan, "'9 to 5' Combines the Talents of Jane and Dolly," *Austin American Statesman*, February 1, 1979, B11.

19. Nat Hentoff, "Cosmo Listens to Records," *Cosmopolitan*, September 1977, 40.

20. Dave Marsh, "The Flip Sides of '79," *Rolling Stone*, December 22, 1979, 28.

Chapter Ten: Glossed in Space

1. Ann Marie Lipinski, "Nancy's 'New Look'—A Democratic Makeover: Magazine Gives Nancy 'New Look,'" *Chicago Tribune*, May 6, 1982, D1.

2. Marian Christy, "Which Look? Street or Sweet," *Boston Globe*, February 11, 1980, 25.

3. Anne Roiphe, "Eye Makeup and the Dark, Mysterious Side of Eros," *New York Times*, January 16, 1980, C1.

4. Elaine Woo, "People Need to Create Some Other Mythic Time," *Los Angeles Times*, May 27, 1984, WS1.

5. Lynn Langway, Linda R. Prout, and Joe Contreras, "The Rockabilly Revolution," *Newsweek*, January 3, 1983, 54–55.

6. "Who Needs Dynasty Pantyhose?" *Tallahassee Democrat*, October 4, 1984, 29.

7. "Shoppers Get a Feast of Carrington Style," *Detroit Free Press*, December 16, 1984, 37.

8. "'Dynasty' Duds Sparkle, but the Sales Are Dull," *Detroit Free Press*, February 17, 1985, 73.

9. "Cosmetics Face the Future," *Newsday*, February 8, 1981, 69.

10. "How to Look Sensational on Your Way Up," *Harper's Bazaar*, March 1980, 188–89.

11. "How to Look Sensational on Your Way Up," 188–89.

12. "Beauty in Action," *Vogue*, February 1, 1980, 274, 275, 276, 277, 278, 279, 280, 281, 282, 283.

13. Stephen Beverly, "Pink Collar Workers Getting Organized," *Boston Globe*, February 13, 1980, 57.

14. "Cosmonauts Pass within 3 Miles: Russian Gal, Man Continue in Orbit," *Pittsburgh Press*, June 17, 1963, 1.

15. Ellen Hale, "Sally to Take Mascaraless Shuttle Ride," *Evening Press*, June 16, 1983, 1.

16. Hale, "Sally to Take Mascaraless Shuttle Ride," 1.

17. Barbara Cloud, "Fashion Videos," *Pittsburgh Press*, October 13, 1985, E1.

18. Mary Rourke, "Fashion: Video TV Rocks 'n' Rolls Its Way as a Style Setter for Streetwear," *Los Angeles Times*, February 24, 1984, G1.

19. Jonathan Takiff, "Ant & Co., Exporters," *Philadelphia Daily News*, February 20, 1984, 29.

20. Lynn Van Matre, "The Talented Mr. George O'Dowd Does Not Want to Be a Woman, OK?" *Chicago Tribune*, April 22, 1984, K18.

21. Lewis Grizzard, "The Boy George Theory," *Atlanta Constitution*, April 20, 1984, 2A.

22. Tom Popson, "The Insider: Poison: Pretty in Pink, Aqua, Peach and Glitter," *Chicago Tribune*, July 3, 1987, FH.

23. J. D. Considine, "Rocking Out This Summer? Then Dress to Excess," *Miami Herald*, July 20, 1988, 35.

Chapter Eleven: Smells Like Teen Lipstick

1. Tina Gaudoin, "Petal Pushers," *Harper's Bazaar*, October 1992, 182–87.

2. Jonathan Poneman, "Grunge & Glory," *Vogue*, December 1, 1992, 254, 255, 256, 257, 258, 259, 260, 261, 262, 263, 313.

3. Lauren Spencer, "Grrrls Only: From the Youngest, Toughest Daughters of Feminism—Self-Respect You Can Rock To," *Washington Post*, January 3, 1993, C1.

4. Joe Whelan, "Grunge, Red Lipstick Set to Expire in the New Year," *Albany Democrat-Herald*, January 1, 1996, 1.

5. Ann Japenga, "Grunge 'R' Us: Exploiting, Co-opting and Neutralizing the Counterculture," *Los Angeles Times*, November 14, 1993, SM26.

6. Matthew Gilbert, "What a Drag. Is Crossdressing Crossing over to the Mainstream?" *Boston Globe*, March 21, 1993, 69.

7. "Fashion Briefs: Eye-Catching Selections," *Daily Record*, October 20, 1996, W2.

8. Cyndee Miller, "Would You Buy Lipstick from This Man?" *Marketing News*, September 11, 1995, 1.

9. Vanessa Friedman, "Health & Beauty: The Image Makers," *Vogue*, January 1, 1996, 132, 133, 134, 136, 137, 181, 182, 183.

10. Kathryn Keller, "Hollywood's Biggest Beauty Secret," *Redbook*, August 1996, 41.

11. Gale Hansen, "Bobbi Tells All," *Harper's Bazaar*, February 1997, 82.

12. Ann Oldenburg, "Market Responds Slowly to a Growing Population," *USA Today*, March 1998, 09D.

13. Alan Patureau, "*Latina, Si* Have Hispanic Women Covered," *Atlanta Journal-Constitution*, July 11, 1996, E01.

14. Nely Galan, "Latin Class," *Vogue*, August 1, 1997, 166, 168, 170.

15. "Bytes: Cosmetic Approach," *Morris County Daily Record*, July 28, 1996, L.

16. Faye Brookman, "Beauty Report 2: Beauty Gets Wired into Computer Age," *Women's Wear Daily*, December 22, 1995, 7.

17. Brookman, "Beauty Report 2," 7.

18. Marisa Fox, "Cyber-Bound Beauty," *Harper's Bazaar*, September 1995, 225, 228.

19. Anne-Marie Schiro, "Can This Face Sell a Million Lipsticks?" *New York Times*, May 30, 1995, B7.

Chapter Twelve: The You Tube

1. "Red Rules," *Ladies' Home Journal*, February 2000, 20.

2. "How to Be a 21st-Century Fox," *Cosmopolitan*, January 2000, 188–95.

3. Eric Randall, "The 'Death of Irony,' and Its Many Reincarnations," *Atlantic*, September 9, 2011, www.theatlantic.com/national/archive/2011/09/death-irony-and-its-many-reincarnations/338114/.

4. Julie Naughton, "Shaken Beauty Market Sets Strategies for Tough First Half," *Women's Wear Daily*, December 14, 2001, 1, 10, 12.

5. "Avon: Cosmetics Firm Will Update 113-Year-Old Image; Focus on Internet," *Courier-Post*, January 23, 2000, 6D.

6. Courtney Kane, "Using Real Women and Believable Promises, Avon Tries a New Way of Advertising Beauty Products," *New York Times*, February 22, 2002, C4.

7. Sally Beatty, "Avon Is Set to Call on Teens," *Wall Street Journal*, October 17, 2002, B1.

8. Stuart Elliott, "Lancôme to Rely Less on the Rose and More on a Bold Signature," *New York Times*, July 6, 2004, C5.

9. Claudia Deutsch, "A Venerable Cosmetics Line Seeks to Freshen Its Appeal," *New York Times*, July 12, 2004, C8.

10. Bryn Kenny, "The It List: P.R. Agencies," *Women's Wear Daily Beautybiz*, April 1, 2004, 38.

11. Peter Jaret, "Dear Web Log: Hated the Shampoo, Loved the Soap," *New York Times*, March 23, 2006, G3.

12. "Whose Lipstick," *Chicago Tribune*, September 10, 2008, 4.

13. Christopher Twarowski, "Biden Targets Female Voters in VA," *Washington Post*, September 20, 2008, A3.

14. Leslie Ryan, "'Simple Life' New Reality at Fox Studio," *TV Week*, February 15, 2004, https://web.archive.org/web/20040215040316/http://www.tvweek.com/topstorys/112403simplelife.html.

15. Melissa Gagliardi, "Pretty in Pink," *Courier-Journal*, April 18, 2004, H3.

16. "How to Trick or Treat As a Celebrity," *Courier-Post*, October 12, 2012, 2D.

17. Stephanie Salzman, "A Brief History of the Failed Kardashian Beauty Brands No One Ever Talks About," Fashionista.com, August 30, 2018, https://fashionista.com/2018/08/failed-kardashian-businesses-beauty-brands.

18. Ruth La Ferla, "A Muse Called Instagram: Designers Are Using It to Get into the Heads of Their Fans, and Vice Versa," *New York Times*, September 15, 2013, ST1.

19. Lavanya Ramanathan, "Ready for Their Close Ups: With 'Full Beat' Videos, YouTube Gurus Draw Fans Wanting to Master the 'Instagram Look,'" *Washington Post*, February 14, 2018, C1–C2.

20. Ramanathan, "Ready for Their Close Ups," C1–C2.

21. "Top Beauty Influencers of 2017," Forbes.com, www.forbes.com/top -influencers/beauty/#3b0507453378.

22. Chase Peterson-Withorn, "Kylie Jenner Is Still the Youngest Self-Made Billionaire in the World," *Forbes*, April 7, 2020, www.forbes.com/sites/chase withorn/2020/04/07/kylie-jenner-is-still-the-youngest-self-made-billionaire-in -the-world/?sh=4b379b9f198b.

23. Amy Zimmerman, "How Kylie Jenner and Khloe Kardashian Profit off Black Creativity," *Daily Beast*, June 12, 2017.

24. Jessica Andrews, "Diversity Report: Magazine Covers in 2015 Weren't as Inclusive as You Think," The Fashion Spot, December 9, 2015, www.thefashion spot.com/Runway-News/667129-Model-Diversity-Report-2015-Magazine -Covers.

25. Karen Grigsby Bates, "Former 'Ebony' Publisher Declares Bankruptcy, and an Era Ends," NPR: Code Switch, April 13, 2019.

26. "Flash Points," *Allure*, October 2016, 110.

27. Ray A. Smith, "Beauty Brands Focus on Women of Color," *Wall Street Journal*, July 14, 2019.

28. Smith, "Beauty Brands Focus on Women of Color."

29. Sandra E. Garcia, "They Couldn't Find Beauty Tutorials for Dark Skin. So They Made Their Own," *New York Times*, November 30, 2018, www.nytimes .com/2018/11/30/style/dark-skin-black-beauty-bloggers-instagram-youtube .html.

30. Danielle Kurtzelben, "7 Ways the U.S. Population Is Changing," *US News*, May 13, 2011, www.usnews.com/news/articles/2011/05/13/7-ways-the -us-population-is-changing.

31. Michelle Ruiz, "Becoming AOC," *Vanity Fair*, December 2020, www .vanityfair.com/news/2020/10/becoming-aoc-cover-story-2020.

32. Joseph Longo, "'Rupaul's Drag Race' Keeps Focus on Art, Not Its Im- pact," *Philadelphia Tribune*, August 17, 2017, 1B.

33. Longo, "'Rupaul's Drag Race' Keeps Focus on Art," 1B.

Epilogue

1. Bethany Biron, "Masks May Be Causing a Blow to Lipstick Sales, but Eye Makeup Sales Are Booming as Americans Find Creative Ways to Use Cosmet-

ics," *Business Insider*, August 11, 2020, www.businessinsider.com/eye-makeup
-sales-rise-lipstick-dips-due-to-mask-wearing-2020-8.

2. Jessica Rapp, "Are Heels Over? What the Footwear Market Will Look
Like Post-Coronavirus," Glossy, August 18, 2020, www.glossy.co/fashion/are
-heels-over-what-the-footwear-market-will-look-like-post-coronavirus.

3. Rapp, "Are Heels Over?"

4. Ilise S. Carter, "Soon You'll Be Able to Print Your Own Lipstick
at Home," *Shondaland*, March 18, 2020, www.shondaland.com/live/beauty/
a31704001/soon-youll-be-able-to-print-your-own-lipstick-at-home/.

5. Carter, "Soon You'll Be Able to Print Your Own Lipstick."

6. Jenny Bailly, "It Was a Pretty Package," *Allure*, April 2020, www.allure
.com/story/beauty-industry-packaging-waste.

7. Cotton Codinha, "Sorry, but You're Not Recycling Beauty Products
as Much as You Think," *Allure*, April 28, 2020, www.allure.com/story/beauty
-products-packaging-recycling-tips.

8. Jillian Mock, "Palm Oil Is in Half of Your Groceries and Destroys Forests.
Can We Fix That?" May 21, 2020, www.huffpost.com/entry/palm-oil-defores
tation-environment_n_5ec389f9c5b682cbd709616d.

9. Sara Bauknecht, "Lip Service? Beauty Industry Called to Go beyond Saying 'Black Lives Matter,'" *Pittsburgh Post-Gazette*, July 13, 2020, D1.

10. Dianna Mazzone, "Beauty by Numbers," *Allure*, February 2021, http://
ezproxy.nypl.org/login?url=https://www.proquest.com/magazines/beautynumbers/
docview/2478784007/se-2?accountid=35635.

11. Michelle Cheng, "Women Are Making over the Beauty Industry's Boys
Club," *Fivethirtyeight*, August 1, 2017, https://fivethirtyeight.com/features/
women-are-making-over-the-beauty-industrys-boys-club/.

12. Pavitrha Mohan, "Can the Beauty Industry Make over the Gender Norms
It Created?" *Fast Company*, June 21, 2018, www.fastcompany.com/40584028/
can-the-beauty-industry-make-over-the-gender-norms-it-created.

13. Riley R. L., "Beauty Brands Want to Sell Queer Expression, but It
Shouldn't Be for Sale," *Teen Vogue*, October 21, 2019, www.teenvogue.com/
story/beauty-brands-queer-expression-makeup.

INDEX